# NAVAJO

## A JOURNEY OF STRENGTH, COURAGE & RESILIENCE

Darryl Benally, Ed.D.

Warrior Psychological Counseling, LLC
Gallup, New Mexico

Warrior Psychological Consulting, LLC
1040 Patton Dr.
Gallup NM, 87301

Cover design by: J.L. Woodson woodsoncreativestudio.com
Interior Design: Lissa Woodson macrompg.com
Editor(s): Stephanie M. Freeman stephaniemfreemanauthor.com
  Naleighna Kai naleighnakai.com
Book Coach: U.M. Hiram authorumhiram.com
Betas: D. J. Mitchell, Christine Pauls, and Marie McKenzie

# NAVAJO

## A JOURNEY OF STRENGTH, COURAGE & RESILIENCE

To my wife and sons
To my father, mother, sister, grandparents,
uncles, aunts, and cousins.
To all my extended family and friends.

While going through the re-writing of my memoir, my younger sister, Renee Benally, was murdered. Out of respect for her and Navajo traditional beliefs, I had to take a brief pause in my writing. Unfortunately, my sister became a statistic in the high rate of missing and murdered Indigenous women in the United States and Canada. This book is primarily dedicated to her because she was not just another statistic. She was my baby sister and a very beautiful woman taken too early.

# ♦ ACKNOWLEDGMENTS ♦

My writing journey began when I joined Naleighna Kai's challenge to write a book in thirty days which I came across on an audio-only app—Clubhouse. Being a school psychologist with a doctorate, my writing was clinical and academic in nature, and never thought I could write a book. I was assigned a daily word count and given my marching orders. My book coach, U.M. Hiram, guided me through the process and helped me believe anything was possible.

Naleighna mentioned writing our stories is a healing process as we revisit and heal from our past traumatic experiences. As we put pen to paper, we address our trauma and turn those experiences into our strengths. The belief is that someone may relate to our stories which can bring them hope. This has certainly been my experience as a wrote this memoir.

After finishing the thirty-day challenge, it was difficult to revisit this piece because I wrote about my younger sister before her passing. NK's Tribe Called Success helped me beyond words that cannot be expressed. They took me under their wing, adopting me as one of their own, and helped me through the healing process with moral, spiritual, and monetary support. As a member of the Navajo Nation, I was blessed to find another tribe.

To my family: Without my family, I would be who I am today. My family sacrificed when I served in the U.S. Army and furthered my education. They were there for me without a doubt.

To my friends: Thank you for your support. I had the opportunity to meet a lot of good people in my life who helped me to become who I am.

To Naleighna Kai: Thank you for being the leader and mentor of NK's Tribe Called Success. Your encouragement and guidance have been invaluable and important to my development as a writer.

I greatly appreciate the sacrifices and advocacy you do on our behalf.

To Stephanie Freeman: Thank you for editing my book and believing in me. I greatly appreciate how you refined and polished my book.

To U.M. Hiram: Thank you for being my book coach as I completed the thirty-day challenge. You were there for me in every step and provided a lot of encouragement. I was never alone for you were a text message or phone away when I needed help.

To D.J. Mitchell, Christine Pauls, and Marie McKenzie: Thank you for helping my book to meet the industry standard and expectations of the consumer. Your feedback was heartfelt and made me a better writer.

To J.L. Woodson: Thank you for graphically developing my cover. You took the time to listen to my wants and needs bringing my book to life. You are the epitome of professionalism and customer service.


While going through the re-writing of my memoir, my younger sister, Renee Benally, was murdered. Out of respect for her and Navajo traditional beliefs, I had to take a brief pause in my writing. Unfortunately, my sister became a statistic in the high rate of missing and murdered Indigenous women in the United States and Canada. This book is primarily dedicated to her because she was not just another statistic. She was my baby sister and a very beautiful woman taken too early.

*"When you were born, you cried, and the world rejoiced. Live your life so that when you die, the world cries and you rejoice."*
Navajo Saying, Author Unknown

# CHAPTER 1

*Capture her... Kill her...*

*Capture her... Kill her...*

*Hania raced through the blinding thickness of trees as the attackers followed. Hoofbeats from their black and brown horses created a thick, choking cloud of dust that billowed around them. The sound of the horses snorting behind her, putting maximum effort into their chase, forced her to break into a swifter run. For all she knew, they had wiped out the rest of her clan. She could not let them kill her too.*

*Early that morning, they'd stolen into the quiet village wearing their traditional buckskins and war colors, the eagle feathers in their hair twisting in the breeze. The stories of this type of horror all ended the same way. Shadows loomed on the horizon before the screaming began. Urgent prayers to The Holy People for protection followed. Most went unanswered. Armed with bows and arrows, the invaders took what they wanted and killed countless of her people before slinking back out of the village with spears drenched in blood and sorrow.*

*Adrenaline spread through her veins, propelling her forward. The walls of the tall red canyons glistened in the sunlight, but she didn't have an extra moment to appreciate their beauty. She had to make it to the clearing. She hazarded a downward glance at the red dress that draped her willowy frame. It matched the color of the painted desert canyon dust which coated the beadwork she had deftly sewn into place. The dress was so loose on her thin frame, she had to lift the hem to run fast and avoid tripping.*

*Hania sprinted into the clearing, heading for the edge of the canyon, using whatever energy she had left. She exerted her utmost effort during the sprint, energized by the tense moment. She paused, sweaty and out of breath, wondering if she could keep going on. Offering up yet another prayer, and hoping that this time, The Holy People would answer ...*

*"Cut her off at the pass," the enemy leader yelled as two riders hastened their black horses, breaking off to the left attempting to corner her into submission. The brown horses and their masters veered to the right, completing the aggressive circle—while they let loose a victory cry as they blocked her only escape route. Or so they believed.*

*"We have her now. She is not going anywhere."*

*Inwardly, Hania fought the fear that his bellow brought on. She jerked her head toward the steep path leading to one of her favorite places to pray. At once, she sprinted toward the track, ignoring the smug satisfaction on the warriors' faces. They were relentless, closing in tighter, making a point of corralling their prey clear.*

*Hania turned with purpose, then uttered a distinct string of words.*

*"Hózhó náhásdlíí."*

*Since she was a Navajo girl, she'd always used that phrase for closing traditional prayers. Every time those few words moved her soul, because it meant there will be beauty all around.*

*She reached the edge of the canyon and made a quick decision. The enemy blocked her only way out and that gave her two choices: she would die by their hands or choose to die by her own. She uttered a prayer to the Holy People to protect her and ran as fast as she could. As she reached the edge of the cliff, she leaped into the air.*

*Hania expected to plummet to the bottom of the canyon, but instead, a powerful burst of wind caught her dress and blew it upward, creating a canopy above her head, allowing her to glide to the valley below. The Holy People—ancestors who were always watching over her people— had heard her prayer.*

*She landed hard on solid ground without any major injury. She hoped she wasn't the last of her clan, but had to embrace that it might be true. Hania bowed her head, deeply thanking The Holy People for her life, and praying that her family was safe. The destruction she had seen in the village gave her little hope, but even so, a little hope was better than no hope at all.*

*As she dusted off her dress, preparing to run once again, she looked up at her pursuers, who were scattered around the cliff's edge. They shook their weapons in anger and disgust, then turned their horses searching for a fast way to get down to her and continue their pursuit. If any band of evil men was capable of such a thing, it would be them. Hania was certain of it. With a reluctant weight in her soul, she accepted that her escape wasn't over.*

The Navajo Tribe is a matrilineal society passing clan membership through the women. Since The Tó'aheedlíinii Lady was the last female member of the Tó'aheedlíinii clan, she was able to revitalize the clan making it one of the largest Navajo clans. The Tó'aheedlíinii Lady was the epitome of resiliency, faith, and bravery. Those elements remain with the clan to this very day.

War within various tribes resulted in one thing … they tried to wipe The Navajo from the face of this earth. But we're still here. People who are a true testament to what's done in the dark will find its way to the light. Today, I am, a proud member of the Navajo Tribe bringing to light the story of the First Nation and my trials, tribulations, and triumphs. Some people would like to forget what happened to my people then, and decades later when outside invaders set foot on North American soil. This is the original "cancel culture" some would like to forget, and others have whitewashed or downplayed the events in history books.

However, the history books do not give the entire account, especially with people who do not want to acknowledge or hold their ancestors accountable for their actions. If you ever want to know how people—who have experienced atrocities that no human should be subjected to—can bounce back, ask an indigenous person what has been done to them. The ancestors provided indigenous people the strength and wisdom to persevere and push forward no matter what.

My history begins with the Tó'aheedlíinii Lady's leap of faith. My story begins with my own. Within these pages, my raw and unfiltered version of growing up Indigenous on or near the Navajo Reservation will be shared. Some people think indigenous people in the United States do not exist, but we are 1.7 percent of the United States population and in every part of American society. We *are* American History.

As indigenous people, our identities *are woven into the names of cities, states and areas throughout America.* We are often associated with those who live in teepees with no access to technology and the outside world. People typically assume indigenous people still live in a version of the Old West.

We are represented as either savages or some lone figure sitting on a horse with a single tear creasing our cheek or some mascot for a sports team. Rarely, if ever, are we represented truthfully. When someone meets a person like me—clean-cut, freshly pressed clothes, ex-military, and speaks the King's English, they are shocked. People, like myself, live in a modern homes, have advanced degrees, and have lucrative careers. Indigenous people have made great contributions to making society a better place to live for all cultures, not just our own.

Since our values have not been publicized, it is easy to assume we only exist in a historical context. When examining textbooks, we are given a small section that talks about our history, with an overt focus on the conquest instead of the beauty of our culture. We have a lot more to offer than films about cowboys and Indians, stereotypical sports mascots, and the "drunken Indian" image.

Whenever we talked about traditional Navajo ceremonies, my Uncle Johnny would say, *"Our Navajo language and culture matter. It is a direct link to our culture. When we sing Navajo traditional songs in a ceremony, we are retelling our history from the beginning of time."* I think back on my childhood and my family and all they endured and all the wisdom they instilled in me. I think of my grandfather sitting in his favorite chair after a long day's work. I think of my Uncle Johnny and my mother, father, and even my sisters trying desperately to navigate our past and a future unfolding before us.

Within each of them was a story so intricately woven to mine, that even in the times when sadness, addiction, and oppression threatened to claim one or more of us, there was always an underlying sense of love, respect, and honor that resonated within them, and ultimately within me.

Uncle Johnny served in the Army during the Vietnam War and returned home to become a Navajo Nation Police Officer. Later, Uncle Johnny worked at Peabody Coal Mine as a mechanic and then retired. After his retirement, Uncle Johnny became a medicine man (healer) who is as wise as anyone with a medical degree.

"What we do matters in this world, we have a relationship with nature which puts us on a different level with the Creator," he explained. "Our prayers are strong because our people are strong and can handle a lot."

Becoming a Navajo Medicine man takes years of mentorship and internship. Medicine Men take on great responsibility in understanding the Navajo traditional ceremonies and songs. In traditional Navajo society, Medicine People are considered "gurus" because they possess a considerable amount of traditional knowledge based on oral teachings committed to long-term memory.

When they perform a ceremony, they essentially recite *everything* from memory which contributes to their overall intellectual ability. Traditionally trained and orientated Navajo people have a deeply unique belief of how the universe originated, which is different from the Big Bang Theory, or biblical beliefs. This is not to say those systems of thoughts and beliefs are not important, but a traditional belief provides a different perspective.

"It is very important to live a good life and do what is right to stay in harmony," Uncle Johnny explained.

"What does it mean to live a good life?" I asked him at one point.

"It means, you're honoring our ancestors and the Holy People. It is the Holy People who made life possible for the life to begin."

Navajo people passed through three different worlds and into the present fourth world with the aid of the animals and Holy People which are a group of deities. The Navajo believe there are two classes of beings which are the Earth and the Holy People. It is believed the Holy People taught the Earth People how to live the correct way and conduct themselves. They were taught to live in harmony with Mother Earth, Father Sky, as well as animals, plants, and insects.

The Holy People placed four sacred mountains in four different directions with Mt. Blanca to the east *(Alamosa, Colorado)*, Mt. Taylor to the south *(Grants, New Mexico)*, San Francisco Peak to the west *(Flagstaff, Arizona)*, and Mt. Hesperus to the north *(Durango, Colorado)*. The four directions are represented by four colors: White Shell represents the east, Turquoise in the south, Yellow Abalone in the west, and Jet Black in the north.

In general, based on Navajo culture, we emerged from the ancestral lands of the four corners region of New Mexico, Arizona, Utah, and Colorado. This is very different from the belief that Navajo people crossed the Bering Strait and came from Asia.

Navajo clanship has its understanding of how their clans emerged from different parts of the region on the Navajo reservation. Based on traditional knowledge, the Tó'aheedlíinii clan, which is my maternal and primary clan, translated as "Water Flows Together", emerged from Northern New Mexico at the meeting of two rivers which is located at the bottom of the Navajo Dam reservoir.

It brings peace and joy to understand and embrace this origin. Due to centuries of cultural genocide, other ethnicities may not necessarily know the origin of their people. Overall, we are not from another country, but indigenous to North and South America.

So, you can imagine how well it went when we indigenous people were recently referred to in the media as ... "Something Else."

# CHAPTER 2

The sun peered through the soft white window curtains signaling another beautiful warm Arizona day. The pleasant bitter fragrance of fresh coffee and breakfast perfumed the air and then, just like that, the world changed. Suddenly, that confidence and positive feeling turned to disgust as CNN played over a 60-inch LCD screen in my living room with the words "Something Else" taking center stage.

During the 2020 election, in a CNN poll, indigenous people were labeled as "Something Else" in comparison to White, Latino, Black, and Asian voters. This created a considerable amount of backlash in indigenous communities. To be called "Something Else" by a major news outlet was disheartening and created feelings of being ostracized, once again being "canceled" from society.

Having been labeled as "Something Else" gave the notion that the rest of American society and media did not care about indigenous people. In a sense, we were invisible, and our presence and history were not acknowledged. Indigenous people have been on the North American continent for thousands of years.

"It is as if they don't care how good my frybread tastes. I make the best frybread around here," my aunt Lucy explained. "Them people who say that ("Something Else") about us don't know anything about good frybread".

Aunt Lucy makes the best frybread from flour, baking powder, salt, and water, which is then cooked in hot oil. So she speaks from the heart.

The morning sun rose higher in the beautiful Arizona sky as the wonderful scent of frybread filled my aunt's kitchen. This provided a wonderful essence for the soul. My aunt was bothered by the distinction of that label, but in her customary fashion, she tried to make light of it.

"It's better to joke around about something instead of getting worked up. We can't control what people think and say about us," my uncle said in response to finding out the CNN report.

"No matter what they say, we have to keep going and live our lives. I can't worry about the nonsense. I need to worry more about my livestock because they are not going to feed and water themselves. My fence needs to be fixed. The politicians in Washington are not going to repair my fence. I have to do that myself."

My uncle pointed out that we must focus on our priorities despite what the media puts out there. My uncle Johnny countered, "It's best to live in 'Hozho' and not worry about everything in this world. It's best to worry about your family and make sure they have food on the table."

Uncle Johnny elaborated his point, "The concept of living in "Hozho" means being in balance with all aspects of life which includes family, culture, employment, and other responsibilities. It is not worth getting worked up over some dumb standard and comment made by the media."

However, the media has an important role in how people of color are portrayed, and it can negatively shape the views of people who don't look any further than that outlet. They don't realize that Indigenous people also contribute to the political climate to bring change.

"I drive a long way just to go vote. When I get there, I must wait a while," Uncle Johnny said. But no matter the inconvenience he was proud to do so. "When I listen to other things they have to say, I found our relatives experience the same treatment," my aunt added. My uncle and aunt were more concerned that their existence did not matter because it took so long for society to even acknowledge that we are still here.

Though Indigenous people occupied North America centuries before Columbus or any other explorers that came after, set foot on the soil here, Indigenous people only became citizens on June 2, 1942, based on the Indian Citizenship Act of 1924. On August 3, 1948, Indigenous people living on reservations in New Mexico were finally allowed to vote. Miguel Trujillo, Sr., was a Marine World War Two veteran and educator from the Isleta Pueblo who advocated for Indigenous people's rights to vote in New Mexico.

The three-panel court in Santa Fe, New Mexico said "Indigenous people have responded to the need of the country in time of war in a patriotic, wholehearted way, both in furnishing manpower in the military forces and in the purchase of war bonds and patriotic contributions of that character." The court further asked, "Why should they be deprived of their rights to vote because they are favored by the federal government in exempting lands from taxation?"

Being labeled as *something else*, at a time when unrest among people of color was at an all-time high, also minimized indigenous people's political contribution to the United States and fails to acknowledge their sovereignty status. The electoral college votes associated with Arizona played a pivotal role in deciding the next president of the United States. In this sense, our indigenous voices were heard on a national level.

Arizona had traditionally been a Republican state which shifted Democratic in a major election where the country had a nail-biting experience of watching the count of votes come in. The state recently passed a bill limiting the distribution of early voting mail. Voters, such as myself, depend on this early voting system to make sure it counts. This action created a barrier to their ability to exercise their precious rights. Polling places are not situated in locations that are easily accessible to indigenous voters.

We are more than *something else* and our lives, culture, and contributions are just as important as anyone else's. As the original inhabitants of the North American continent, we are trying to make a living and do what is right for our children. Our hope is the next generation will continue to make positive changes and contributions to the world.

Imagine having to live with your identity and heritage being eraised; or worse, having your experiences swept under the carpet because polite society is uncomfortable. And I say the word polite with air quotes because what was done to us was by no means, polite or in harmony and balance by any stretch of any imagination. Their actions were fueled by greed and being dismissive of any people or culture that did not mirror their own.

The boarding school experience of indigenous people is a fine example of Cancel Culture at its best—an attempt to wipe out the oral traditions and histories of our people. Thousands of children were ripped from their homes and subjected to systematic abuse for the "greater good" only to have those experiences concealed in the same manner as the young bodies they buried to cover their crimes. When the public wants us to turn the other cheek, it is easy to forget about a controversial event that stripped children from their parents and thrust them into a place designed to make them forget everything that mattered—who they were and their connection to the Creator.

# CHAPTER 3

*Forget all that you are for the emptiness we provide.*

My first experience attending boarding school began in the Fall of 1980. Most students spoke the Navajo language and were not fluent in English. However, students were forced to speak only English causing them to feel out of place. My entrance to kindergarten was with a strong background in the English language, well ahead of my Navajo-speaking peers.

My mother, a petite raven-haired woman with a heart-shaped face, was employed as a pre-school teacher and exposed me to an English language-based curriculum at an early age. Since my mother did not have a babysitter, she took me with her every day. Current research suggests early childhood education is important for later development. My mother was at the forefront of that research.

The Nenahenzah Boarding School was set against large dirt-based hills displayed as far as the eye could see in both directions. Between the school building, and the hills, large irrigation carried water to various vegetation fields. Large trees which swayed as they caught mild breezes from the wind, were adjacent to the outside of the playground parameter.

On the Navajo Reservation, boarding schools were built in the 1930s with walls and wooden roofs. The main portion of the Nenahenzah Boarding School was constructed at that time. Since the schools were made of stone, the building was naturally cool in the summer and warm in the winter.

Modern editions to boarding schools were initiated in the 1950s. The newer buildings had an eggshell color and were strategically placed to spread out over the overall campus. Sidewalks, which served as walkways, connected the different areas of the school. Boarding school students played basketball on courts with cement floors, not the wooden ones everyone sees today.

Much of the lot was hard-packed dirt without any grass or the vegetation I grew up with on my grandfather's farm. As students trampled on the hard dirt surface, dust typically kicked up that was easily caught adrift in mild breezes.

Every morning, my ultimate dread was going to the place where I was slowly being forced to exchange one culture for one they thought was better, more civilized.

"Are you ready to go?" my mother asked.

"Yeah, I suppose so." Fear crept into my gut at the prospect of another day of torment from my surroundings and the bullies that prowled the schoolyard like wolves. Education was important to my mother and even at an early age, I didn't want to let her down.

"After you finish with breakfast, start the truck," my mother directed, totally unaware of my inner turmoil.

We had a yellow 1975 Ford F150 with an extended cab. Once the ignition choke was pulled to start the engine, a strong puff of exhaust blasted from the tailpipe. A stick had to be propped against the gas pedal to keep the engine from stalling. All this work to get the vehicle moving felt very much the same as trying to get me going.

The teachers at the boarding school were hard on the students, wanting us to learn the English language and forget our own. Students being smacked by thick wooden yardstick rulers was the norm. Fear quickly became a deterrent to attending school and being around another type of trauma. In my kindergarten class, most students spoke Navajo and had difficulty mastering the English language. To this day, I thank my mother for being an educator who taught preschool. Her dedication to my mastery of the English language gave me quite the advantage.

Luckily, this helped me to avoid the punishment which was a welcome respite from the physical abuse I witnessed at home.

Nenahenzah Boarding School held kindergarten through twelfth grades with very limited separation between the students. Kindergarten students were allowed to intermingle with middle and high school students. Since it was a government school, the administration could do as they pleased without regard for promoting a positive and safe school environment. The boarding school had a fixed government budget and used money-saving tactics without taking school safety into account, separating the students, or providing enough adult supervision.

This was most students' first exposure to any type of school environment that would make them feel like an "outsider" than a valued member of society. They were from the reservation ahd had to quickly adapt to being in an educational setting. All I can remember about those early days was a combination of unpleasant smells and the fights that went unchecked by an adult.

My classroom had a particular musky smell very similar to old dirt which collected on a shaggy, yellow 1970s style rug. Old dirt is a matter which settles on a carpet and collects various odors by exposure to so many people. The teaching staff would use a metal Hoover vacuum with a large, burgundy, and black plaid designed bag, to tidy up. Unfortunately, the dirt would win each time and that unpleasant smell lingered.

Teachers and students cleaned their classrooms without relying on custodians, another one of those cost-saving tips and tricks that rarely worked. When approaching the classroom to begin the school day, all I remember was the whirring sound of the vacuum and the sight of the students who were tasked with certain details to help out. The vacuum resembled a large silver ladybug that seemed to chase the other students who were picking up the trash.

Cleaning was not an issue for me since I always helped my grandmother clean around the house. Keeping busy caused me to attract less attention. Teachers paid more attention to students standing around the classroom.

"All right class, let's get ready for breakfast. Put your cleaning supplies away and line up," one raven-haired teacher ordered. At once we scattered to all points of the room to stow our cleaning supplies including cleaning rags, squirt bottles with pine-scented disinfectant, brooms, and the Old Ladybug Vacuum. Once the class complied, the student in front of the line reported, "We are lined up and ready to go."

Before class, we ate breakfast and played on the playground. The cafeteria was a small old portable building that reminded me of an old mobile home or trailer. Breakfast was almost always the same: rubbery powdered eggs with no flavor and burnt sausage fried so hard we could have broken a window if we threw it out.

The kitchen staff was ruthless to students and would bark orders at us as if we were in the military. Mrs. Yazzie stood behind the serving counter in cook whites and a hairnet looking like something out of a nightmare. If she loved her job at any point, those days had long gone. The frown on her face was nothing compared to the way she stood there sweating and swiping at her brow as if serving food was an unwanted chore. Her mean gaze was enough to make anyone feel uncomfortable.

"Hurry up and get in line," Mrs. Yazzie yelled as the children entered the cafeteria and hustled to the food counter. It was common practice for her and the other cafeteria staff to scream at the students to get their point across.

The kitchen staff yelled at us to stay in line, finish our food, and clean up after ourselves as if we didn't have any home training. I didn't know it at the time, but the boarding school staff had the same mentality as military personnel. In retrospect, all that yelling did a considerable amount of damage since it demoralized and made us feel afraid of being in the school cafeteria.

Screaming was used to foster discipline and mental toughness, the same way belittling and breaking down recruits is a process when going through Army Basic Training. Drill sergeants and instructors yell at recruits when entering the military to toughen them up and get them ready for war. Recruits were treated harshly so they would not buckle when in a combat scenario. The screaming scared recruits but prepares them to be under stress.

Just like in boarding school, in the Army, we had to march in a single file and take timed side steps while pushing our cafeteria tray. Drill sergeants were at every corner making sure we kept in step and ate fast. In an Army chow hall, we ate in silence, with a spoon—no fork or knife—feet had to be placed directly under the table, elbows tucked in, and we could only look at our food. If we were caught looking around, we were told to dump our trays because we were considered finished with our meal.

When I think back on my time in boarding school, I believe the kitchen staff was trying to teach the students manners, but they could have done so without screaming at us as if we could not hear or understand. Some children would start crying the minute the first words bounced off the walls. Students took their trays to the cafeteria table with tears streaming down their cheeks. Being yelled at was second nature for me as much as everyone else.

After we were done eating, we were marched to our classroom to begin instruction. The cafeteria staff presented as typical people but were extremely forceful and instilled fear in students as a means of controlling them. It's as if they didn't know any other way.

Parental and community involvement was limited and not supported. Upon entering the boarding school setting, it was a closed environment. Whatever transpired behind those walls remained a mystery to the outside world. The walls hid the truth about the traumatic abuse experienced by the children. Perhaps they did not want their inhumane practices to be known by the public. Maybe they did and just didn't care. When federal funds are involved, transparency is a must. Of course, they need to know how their money is being spent, but if that money is supposed to help with the betterment of a marginalized group of children, shouldn't they be just as concerned about the treatment of said children?

That wasn't the case with us.

The boarding school kept everything hidden from the public. No one questioned how children were being mistreated by the school staff or were buried in the hills beyond the schoolyard. We weren't the only ones. Countless other indigenous children across the country and the northern borders of Canada "disappeared" as the school day ground on. No one ever knew what happened to those little ones. The systematic abuse became part of the collected conscious. For us, and our parents before us, everything was crystal clear. No one was coming to save us, so we had no choice but to endure.

At the time, more parents should have made a point to come to the school and inquire about what was being done. Parent involvement did not appear to be a priority at that time. When children reported they were spanked or hit with a ruler, parents did not question those damaging practices. Maybe this could have been prevented with more parents inquiring about what went on during our time away from them. Navajo Tribal officials rarely came onto the boarding school campus, so they were of little help, to begin with.

Little regard was given to promoting a positive school environment where students, parents, and community members felt welcomed. No one asked any hard questions and had full faith in government. They did not have the best interest of Navajo children in mind. The only thing that mattered was money, power, and control.

Students were brutal to each other in such an unsupervised setting. This included places behind buildings and anywhere on the playground and out of sight from school personnel. Middle school students beat up younger students in that large open area with old metallic playground equipment.

Since most students spoke Navajo fluently and my language skills leaned toward a better command of English, making friends was a challenge. This put me at a disadvantage in creating meaningful relationships, and also at a loss of not being as proficient in Navajo as my peers and making important relationships. One middle-school-aged student befriended me and allowed me to hang out with him while doing my best to copy and learn Navajo. This is one of the best memories I have of that place.

Little did I know, my mother had an experience within those walls that far overshadowed what I endured.

# CHAPTER 4

The Tó'aheedlíinii Lady was the last best hope of her people. When she stole away into the canyon that fateful day, more than likely, she was following the instructions the elders gave all of the children when invaders spilled into their village with bloodlust in their eyes.

*If we cannot fight them off, then go where I send you. Conceal yourself in the walls of the canyons. Flee this place. Find safety and shelter elsewhere.*

One day during recess, I found my new friend broken, bloody, and stretched out on the ground.

"Hey, are you all right?" I asked, already knowing that he wasn't. "What happened?"

"They accused me of taking their Hot Wheels cars from the dorm. I told them I didn't have any cars, but they beat me up anyway. I tried running away from them, but they caught up to me," he replied. "Hey, help me up, I need to go to the bathroom and clean myself up. Do I have a black eye?"

"Yeah, you sort of look like Rocky after a title fight. Next time, you should run faster," one of the other kids teased.

Somehow, word got back to the teachers, and those bullies came looking for my friend. The second he saw them walking in our direction, he was out of there! I didn't blame him. I hated seeing my friend suffer, but it was open season on the playgrounds and the bullies ruled the roost.

Most traveled in packs and tormented those of us too weak to run or fight back. Part of me was furious at the teachers showing up after the fact, but then it was all too familiar. Back home, I had another bully to contend with in the form of my father. To say my relationship with my father was complicated is an understatement. There were times when I wondered if he loved me and then there are the moments when the skills, he taught me served me well.

I always wondered what went through their minds as the bullies terrorized the other students. As a child, they were no better than the monsters we imagined were hiding in our closets. As an adult, I look back and think about how it gave them the power to intimidate and terrorize people who could not fight back. Part of me wondered if they had bullies at home too.

During recess, some students would play with toy cars and the bullies blatantly grabbed them, declaring they belonged to them without any regard or empathy for the original owners of the toys. I made it a point to leave my Hot Wheels cars at home. It was better to play alone than to deal with the prospect of my toys being stolen.

Growing up, my father taught me to hunt wild game, so I put my hunting skills to use by scoping out and avoiding the main quartet of gangsters. Once the bullies were spotted, it was easy to discretely become incognito. We had to stay one step ahead of them to avoid being terrorized. I quickly learned that if you were wise, you didn't cry. Tears were like blood in the water. Those boys lurked around every corner like sharks in the ocean looking for their next prey. Often, they would hit and knock students over and caused their victims to land hard on the ground. Then would stand back and laugh. But when they were reported to the teachers, those bullies would run away like cowards.

In Navajo culture, we have a clan system which is how we identify with the environment and each other. Each Navajo person has four clans with the primary being the mother and father's clan. In this manner, we develop a relationship with other Navajo people if we have similar clans. It is the same as carrying an identification card. Once we introduce ourselves with our names and clans, other Navajo people can instantly connect with that person and there is harmony and balance in this peaceful action.

Somehow, I doubt if the bullies got that memo. Most of them were probably related to their victims. Clan identity and other indigenous methods were not supported at the boarding school. Children mirror what they see, and this new environment presented an "ugly" reflection of separation and divisiveness.

The bullies found pleasure and enjoyment in their actions. Hence, just like staff, the bullies enjoyed having a state of power over younger and vulnerable students. The younger students had no choice but to accept and adapt to the reality that the boarding school staff did not have their safety and best interests at heart.

During some of the worst experiences I had at the boarding school, my father was always somewhere in the background. One week, he took me to see "Animal House" starring John Belushi. The scene with the food fight still makes me smile. I remember thinking about starting a major food fight to protest against our treatment, but as quickly as the thought entered my mind, it left. The last thing I wanted was the undivided attention of a teacher or staff member that had no problem smacking our hands with their wooden rulers. But my father was there, and while home life could be just as brutal, there were times when he would step in and be the parent I needed, instead of the one I had.

One morning my father took me to school, and I couldn't keep the tears from streaming down my face.

"How come you're crying? You're not supposed to be crying, you're supposed to be tough. So, what's going on?"

"Some are students giving me a hard time. One of my friends was beaten up pretty bad," I replied.

"I don't like you crying, I am going to come with you, and you show me which kids are picking on you," he insisted.

He stormed onto the playground that day in search of the boys who tormented me. In that instant, pride and sheer terror pulsed through my veins and warred for equal amounts of space. On a good day, my father's adventurous spirit was like sunshine warming me from the inside out. When it was bad, the best anyone could do was take cover as his wrath ripped through our home.

My father could be unpredictable and might physically attack the students. Here it is, as we patrolled the playground, I found myself suddenly afraid for the bullies who hurt others daily. They must have sensed something, or maybe they saw his fists clenched and ready for war. At first, the bullies were nowhere to be found. However, one finally appeared.

"Well? Is that him?" he snapped.

Terror ripped through me. Back then, on the Navajo Reservation, laws did not exist for protecting students. An adult could easily confront students on the playground with no teacher to intervene. Adults could have easily kidnapped one of us or beat us to a bloody pulp and not one single adult would notice.

"Are you the one picking on my boy?" he roared. My father, who was tall like my grandfather, cast a large shadow, practically towering over the child like the Jolly Green Giant plucking a cob of corn from the valley.

The kid tried to make a run for it. Unfortunately, my father grabbed him by the arm, yanking him back, almost in the same way a cowboy ropes a calf. I felt sorry for him.

"Mommy," the boy wailed still dangling from my father's fist like a discarded rag doll.

"You better leave my son alone or I will be back. Do you hear me?" He punctuated each word with a shake that made the boy scream even more.

My father eventually let him go and he quickly took off. Luckily, the whistle blew at that moment, alerting students that school was about to begin. A big lump formed in my throat as I hurried off to class. Some members of the teaching staff had observed my father and did not question or confront him. It was one thing to experience my father's wrath at home, but to see it on full display in public terrified me even more.

The bullies quickly learned of my father's actions after one of their own fell into the crosshairs of my father's rage. Afterward, they left me alone because they knew my father would come looking for them. Just like the teachers didn't come to our rescue, no one was going to save them once my father showed up.

As an adult, nightmares still haunt me about my boarding school experience. The song, "On the Road Again," by Willie Nelson, serves as a reminder of my time in boarding school. Just the song itself brings back the emotions and feelings associated with the setting. The faces of the students and familiar smells of the boarding school haunt the quiet places in my mind.

Looking back, it is difficult to understand how someone could find happiness in such a hell hole. Some students loved the boarding school because they had the personality for the setting. Others, to this day, are probably still recovering. Boarding school students lived nearly one hundred miles away from their homes and had to be bussed to those locations.

A lot of students from the reservation did not have access to electricity or running water. Homes were heated by woodstoves and mostly used oil lanterns for light. The family of the children hauled water for basic uses.

If you were to ask many of the parents who sent their children to those places some would shrug away the shame while others would meet your gaze. They would say: *What choice did we have? With no electricity and no running water, what would you have done? Public schools were miles away from border towns. How would we get them there in the winter when the roads were impassible? At least when they were away at the boarding school, they would be taken care of. What was there to come home to?*

In the boarding school setting, at least students were able to wash their clothes, have access to electricity and running water, and have food to eat even if that food was practically unbearable. For some students, boarding school food was a luxury because poverty was rampant. Thankfully, that wasn't my experience, but others were not so fortunate.

My purpose has never been to seek recognition as a boarding school survivor. So many other Indigenous people had it harder than me. When we peel back the layers of history, we can see that even the smaller ecosystem was designed to destroy the Navajo language and culture early on. Instead of preparing us to enter society equipped with skills and abilities that would help improve our situations, this was another way to erase us.

In retrospect, I realize that all of this combined means one major thing: The Tó'aheedlíinii Lady's leap of faith is proof. We were meant to be here.

# CHAPTER 5

Jekyll and Hyde tended the fields just as we did ...


Normally when people hear that word, *reservation*, they think of teepees as far as the eye can see, and stoic men astride massive steeds forever staring into the West where those shadows grow. Generations ago perhaps that was true. Navajo clans have evolved since The Tó'aheedlíinii Lady's time. When I think of my boyhood home, I think of Upper Fruitland.

The entire community was farmland filled with people actively growing alfalfa, vegetables, and fruit trees on the land. Compared to other portions of the reservation, Upper Fruitland was an oasis with a wonderful scent of vegetation.

Water for the fields came from the San Juan River. Looking to the north, the scene was green from all the adjacent and connecting fields. To the north, La Plata Mountain was visible in the background.

Across the river is Kirtland, New Mexico, which was off the reservation. The San Juan River separates Upper Fruitland from Kirtland, where stores, gas stations, a post office, laundromats, small stores, and public schools exist.

Large hills, which were more like small mountains, bordered my grandparents' farm in the south. A huge irrigation ditch separated the homestead from the large hills. Other farms were present on either side of my grandparents' farm with relatives occupying most of the farming area.

Cottonwood trees grew to tower heights near my grandparents' farm and attracted several different species of birds. The music of my days and nights began and ended with the crisp melody of the birds and the twelve horses that roamed the area.

Even with all that peace and serenity surrounding me, substance abuse—like the invaders that pursued The Tó'aheedlíinii Lady—was a major problem in my household. In the 1970s and 1980s, alcohol was readily available to anyone that wanted to escape the rigors of life in general. With poverty levels skyrocketing, being "elsewhere" wasn't a location, it was an ideal. Men and women turned to alcohol and other drugs to self-medicate when the pain of their reality became too much to bear.

*It wasn't the first time.*

Historically, alcohol was utilized by the Eurocentric invaders and settlers to tame the Indigenous people. During trading with the tribes, alcohol give an edge to the settlers who sought to have animal skins and other valuable resources. Alcohol changed Indigenous people. When they were under the influence, many made poor decisions and became violent.

My father was no exception. He fell victim to the "alcohol spirit" which took total control of his life. The alcohol spirit is unforgiving and does not care whom it consumes. The happy and healthy father I loved and respected became a stranger when he drank. Eventually, alcohol became more important than the health and well-being of his family.

His alcohol-induced transformation was much like Dr. Jekyll and Mr. Hyde. While under the influence, he was not able to rationalize, make adequate decisions, or control his anger. My mother bore the brunt of that anger along with the children they brought into this world who couldn't understand why that wonderful human being had disappeared.

Being a heavy diesel mechanic meant my father had rank and privileges that usually ended up with an invitation to the bar with his coworkers. Night after night, my older sister and I cringed as the loud music blasted and the fighting would begin.

For Indigenous people, alcohol is not easily digested leading to health problems and addiction. While father did his best to support the family, alcohol took center stage and ruined our lives. I cannot tell you how many families are destroyed because of alcoholism.

A child had no place in trying to correct the behaviors of their parents, but that appeared to be my lot in life. Naturally, a young boy wants to protect his mother regardless of the social situation. Perhaps that is the reason they are not afraid to defend their mothers from their attacking fathers.

*Stay out of it. Your parents fighting is not your fault. They are adults and have to figure things out. Once they start fighting, you should come to our house where it is safe.*

Every time my parents fought, those words flowed through my head as softly as my grandmother's hands reached out to provide comfort. My grandparents knew what was going on but feared for our safety if we tried to intervene.

My parents married young, not long after they graduated from high school. They may not have been equipped and mature enough to start a family. My mother initially started at the University of New Mexico in the early 1970s but withdrew when she gave birth to my older sister. My father was drafted into the United States Army and reported to Fort Bliss, Texas, for in-processing. However, he was considered "unfit for service" because he injured his knee playing football which required surgery. Instead, Father enrolled at New Mexico State University in Las Cruces, New Mexico.

After a hard night of drinking, my father was not going to put up with being questioned by my mother. It was easier for him to lay his hands on my mother versus putting up with her. My mother experienced a considerable amount of physical, emotional, and financial abuse at the hands of my father. During that time, in the 1970s through the 1980s, women experienced a significant amount of abuse but rarely reported it. Women's shelters that protected abusive partners were nowhere to be found on the Navajo Reservation. The Navajo legal system did not provide adequate security for my mother and other women who were experiencing the same situation. Unfortunately, abused women and children did not typically have a designated safe place.

People always wanted to present a positive image of the families but only so much could be hidden behind closed doors. Some of us knew what was happening as bruises and black eyes always were at the forefront. Spousal abuse against women was more socially acceptable back then.

Domestic violence continues to be as much of a concern today as it was in my youth. Some have described domestic violence as a dark cloud that brings sadness to happy families. I, for one, can attest to that. Sadness is a sickness that infects everyone it touches.

We lived in a 1970s era single trailer mobile home with three bedrooms. The trailer was an eggshell white, with large brown trim on the edges. On the south side, my parents had a large master bedroom with an adjacent bathroom. The northern portion consisted of the living room, two small bedrooms, and a bathroom.

On a particularly violent night of fighting between my parents, I ventured out to see what was going on and found my mother was bleeding. When it became horrible, I would run to my grandparents' house. They would come over and defuse the situation.

Once my mother had the presence of mind to escape. Latching onto my father's leg, I tripped him which bought time for my mother to take my infant sister into the bathroom. The next thing I knew, my father had thrown me across the living room. My head cracked on a barbell weight on the floor. I was small for my age, but tough—even at six years old. If nothing else, growing up around my grandfather and his horses taught me how to fall. That night the skill served me well. My mother and little sister were able to fit through a small bathroom window to escape. My father eventually broke the door down and tossed me aside.

One of the neighbors called the Navajo Police. I was relieved when that white cruiser with the Navajo Police emblem on the doors with red and blue magnetic lights on the roof came into view.

*Everything is okay now. The police are here!* As a 6-year-old, I understood the police were there to help the people by putting the bad guys in jail. My mother would be protected and maybe my father would get the help he needed too. With the authorities involved, surely the fighting would stop. Maybe we could even be a family again and anything and everything would be okay because an officer of the law was present.

The officer wore a traditional tan uniform with the covenant Navajo Police patch and shiny badge. A heavy knock echoed throughout the house to the bedroom where I awaited the outcome.

When he came to the door, he asked, "What is going on? I was sent here for a disturbance."

My father explained, "Everything is all right. Just having a dispute with my wife."

The police officer told my parents, "You guys better cool it and work it out, you have kids around."

"All right," my father responded.

"Mind if I come inside and have a look around?"

"No, come right in … I was just watching a football game."

My father sounded cheerful as if he wasn't in there throwing me aside like a used garment before breaking down the bathroom door to get to my mother. As the officer inspected our home, I hoped that he could see the path of destruction leading through our home. I prayed he would see the broken dishes and the holes in the walls from the last time my father flew into a rage.

The signs were all there, hanging in the air like a scream, cowering in the corners. He had to *see* it. He had to *feel* it.

"Are you all right?" the officer asked as he moved closer to me.

I didn't even bother to look in my father's direction. I already knew he had "the look" on his face, almost daring me to speak up. This was family business after all, and families took care of their own. Cop or not this man was not family. Would never be family and the best thing for all involved, including me, was to say nothing. Anything else meant more pain later for my mother, for me, and maybe even my sisters. Because they never stayed locked up for long. Eventually, the abusive parent came home filled with remedial and thorough lessons on why it was impolite to share family business with strangers.

I nodded and hoped the officer would take in all that he observed and make the right decision. As the taillights to the cruiser disappeared around a corner, my heart sank. My father got off with a warning and the usual glib advice about sleeping it off. My mother would continue experiencing more of the same. Heading back to my room it dawned on me—if the police officers weren't going to do anything, what did that mean for my mother? What did that mean ... *for us*?

That's when I realized it was time to act and help my mother escape the volatile scene. She waited until my father drifted off then gathered what little she could and left to be with my grandparents.

Eventually, we all went to my grandparents' house to stay, and I was glad. At least with my grandfather present, my father would not be allowed to enter their home being drunk and abusive. Supervillains and heroes all had a weak spot. Any kid, even the bullies from boarding school knew that. When I think back on those days when Jekyll and Hyde walked into our house trailer in the form of my father, I remember my hero walked there too.

My grandfather was more powerful than the police.

# CHAPTER 6

Whenever Grandfather spoke, my father listened and never questioned his teaching and guidance. My father had a lot of respect for the older man, even in his drunken state. Father intended to stay on positive terms with him at all costs.

Navajo men tended to be short, but Grandfather, a rancher, was a tall man with short hair tucked under a cowboy hat. Back in his younger days, Grandfather rode saddle bronc in the rodeo circuit but retired and went into horse racing.

When World War II came calling, his generation enlisted and traveled to Europe and the South Pacific taking on the cause of America's interests against the German and Japanese Empires. He followed in his older brother's footsteps volunteering for the Marine Corps feeling the need to defend our homeland. They did not back down and wanted to do their part to stop the spread of hate. Sadly, they couldn't combat the hate that was closer to home.

Upon his entry into the Marine Corps, Grandfather was sent to boot camp and then to Code Talker school. The brave Navajo Marines utilized a code based on the Navajo language in the South Pacific Theater to send special messages between units. Rather than talk about his war experiences, my grandfather chose to address his post-traumatic stress disorder the way many of his generation did. Meaning, he didn't. He kept no souvenirs from his time behind enemy lines and didn't own anything with the Marine Corps Emblem.

Although Grandfather only went to the eighth grade, he knew how to invest and handle his money well. He worked his way up to a foreman at the Navajo Mine—Utah International and supervised a crew of men. Other returning "code talkers" also found adequate employment based on their military experience. He advanced in his position at the Navajo Mine. As a role model and leader, he provided mentorship to the people who were under his leadership.

Grandfather had excellent memory which he developed serving as a Navajo Code Talker. He had to memorize code and different ships and tanks associated with the Japanese and American military. While under an excessive amount of combat stress, he delivered code based on working memory alone.

Naturally, grandfather was able to transfer his military skills into civilian life. He was able to understand graphs, schematics, and blueprints, without any training or engineering education. He was an example of how people possess superior intellectual ability without a formal education.

Grandmother, a short, round woman with a wide smile and close-cropped hair, displayed a picture of my grandfather when he went through boot camp, so we knew he was in the Marine Corps. Additionally, we understood the unspoken rule and we did not ask my grandfather any questions about his experiences. Only when I was in high school, did he reveal that he was indeed one of the legendary Code Talkers. I didn't believe him at first.

After finding my grandfather's name in the national Navajo Code Talker archive, only then was my doubt erased. Immediately, this new revelation filled me with pride. Out of respect for his wishes, I did not share this information until now. The world needs to know the important role the Navajo played in American history.

Grandfather was a man of limited words and only spoke when he needed to say something or get his point across. He never verbalized his problems and feelings. However, Grandfather did express concern knowing my father had a severe drinking problem. He respected the household of my parents and never interfered in their affairs unless my sisters and I were in danger. He would offer words of concern, but never imposed his beliefs and views on my parents.

"You better slow down with your drinking and spend more time with your boy," Grandfather warned my father at one point.

"All right dad."

When I discussed things with my grandfather, he shared some personal experiences. For a man who spoke few words, every conversation with him was like a Masterclass. The wisdom he imparted, and the wealth of knowledge he gained from life made him a guru.

"I used to drink a lot of alcohol but understood it was not doing me any good. I decided to put down the bottle and focus on bettering myself and making sure the farm was operating correctly. I had a deep concern for the well-being of my livestock and farming which is more important than drinking alcohol," Grandfather stated.

He was the only one who could quiet the beast that raged in my father with just a few choice words. Never once did he raise his voice. Never needed to. My grandfather would reach him, even moving past the alcohol, the disappointment, and the hidden pain he never talked about. Grandfather spoke to my father's heart.

*I need you to slow down on your drinking and help me fix the tractor. I can't figure out why it has been leaking fluid.*

Father simply listened, but I'm not sure if he "heard" what the old man was trying to say.

Fueled by a need to gain my grandfather's respect, my father replied "Okay, let me grab my tools so that I can take a look at it."

Grandfather cared deeply about his adult children and grandchildren, but it wasn't enough to protect my mother at times. He was concerned for my immediate family and often prayed to the Holy People in the morning, sprinkling white cornmeal towards the morning dawn as an offering for good fortune and safety. Rather than complain and try to take issue with my parents, he prayed. Grandfather had a traditional Navajo belief and often explained: "everything happens for a reason".

As a child, hearing him explain life was soothing to my wounded spirit. Even now when the world crashes in, I listen for my grandfather's voice.

*When hardship happens in life, it's trying to tell you something. That's when you must pray or have a medicine man help you with a prayer. We have our traditions to rely on when life gets hard.*

Grandfather had a large quartz crystal which he believed could show him the problems people experienced. In the crystal, he could "see" the imbalance people were experiencing, on the same level as a spiritual guru. He had a positive connection with the environment and helped put people back on a path of balance and harmony. This didn't work so well for my parents, but then again, some domestic issues are difficult to solve with supernatural intervention alone.

The belief is when we are experiencing problems, we are out of balance and need to be realigned. Once people are back in balance, they become actualized and can continue forward with their lives. I strive for this type of balance since my parents never embraced this concept. Then there came a time in my life when I understood my parents all too well.

# CHAPTER 7

On the reservation, the air of the alfalfa field reflected the omniscient and spiritual presence of the horses. Fine tendrils of sunlight played with the morning dew as a light breeze danced through the cottonwood tree leaves.

Before working with the livestock in the early morning, Grandfather would take a drink of Navajo herbs soaked in water and offered some to me as well. The tea was strong and bitter, much like mixing horseradish with water. The purpose was to make our mind, body, and spirit strong.

My grandfather taught me that horses were animals that emerged from the sun. Horses are spiritual beings requiring the utmost care because they belong to the sun and carry our prayers to the Holy People. Feeding the horses in the morning was always a serene activity. Once we went outside, he sprinkled cornmeal as an offering to the holy spiritual people for prayers, guidance, knowledge, and strength.

On hot summer days, Grandfather's horses had to be constantly watered throughout the day. During the months of June and July, in New Mexico, the temperature could easily hit one hundred degrees Fahrenheit. The large cottonwood trees on my grandparents' farm provided relief from the radiant sun which beat down on my skin. The whistling sound of the leaves could be heard as a crisp breeze quickly passed. Horses made snorting noises as they acknowledged my presence. My responsibility was to keep the five-gallon water buckets filled with fresh water.

Grandfather often encouraged patience when watering the horses allowing them to drink as much as they desired. Often, this was a long process, but in high temperatures horses needed adequate hydration. Much in the same way I craved my grandfather's wisdom to quench the thirst in my soul.

He had brown, black, and white horses that liked me well enough. Honestly, I believe they associated me with being fed and watered. On hot days, the horses looked at me with relief knowing what I brought with me. The horses knew me and provided comfort far away from the troubles at home. Somehow, the horses picked up on my negative vibes about my home environment and spirited them away as they raced across the open fields.

When the day was done, they would settle in the stable ushering in an all-encompassing peace that quieted my soul.

During one of those respites from my parents' home, I could hear my grandparents talking about my father's addiction. Most kids would have been shocked or embarrassed by what was discussed. By this time, I had already seen and heard so much at home that darker parts of our life experience didn't touch me in the way it would another child.

My grandparents referred to my father as 'Junior' as a distinction that my father was his son, and to me as 'Turk.' According to my parents, my first spoken word was Turkey, and my nickname became 'Turk' for that reason.

*I get concerned when Junior drinks too much," Grandmother said. "He seems to like drinking his beer and gets carried away. Turk needs a father, and whether Junior realizes it or not, he needs his son. Children don't remain small forever. If he has no time for them now, they may return the favor as adults. They have to learn how to work things out. I don't want Turk to get hurt when Junior is drinking.*

The disquiet in Grandfather's voice put me at ease. I wanted to tell them my father had already hurt us in so many ways that didn't involve me being thrown across a room, or my mother and sisters cowering in a bathroom.

My grandmother was always sensitive to us. She seemed to know when we were up to mischief or when the questions were too painful to ask out loud. To give me some consolation, Grandmother shared some background of my father's upbringing.

*Your grandpa left your dad, uncle, and aunt with their mom. She drank too. When she did, she would neglect them. Once grandpa found out about this, he went to pick up his children and brought them to Upper Fruitland. Then he asked me to raise your dad, uncle, and aunt.*

Grandmother is my father's stepmother but loved and accepted my father, uncle, and aunt, as her children. She was in a nursing program in the early 1960s and gave it up to raise them. She did her best to teach them how to be good people. Somewhere along the line, alcohol came into the mix, and the good person my father had been, became something else entirely.

My grandmother could have easily said "no" and chose to continue her nursing career, which was her lifelong goal. However, she had a big heart and wanted to help him in raising new members of their family. Grandmother serves as a role model and support for most of our relatives and people in her community.

Grandmother often emphasized that she gave up her career to give us the opportunity of living a good life. Observing your parents fight and argue is not easy to process as a child. She always had a kind way to explain events that were beyond my understanding. She had her way of providing comfort and was deeply concerned with the actions of my parents. She also did her best to maintain an uncomfortable distance. Her primary concern was the safety of me and my sisters.

She raised me and I know that without her guidance, my fate could have been far worse. My placement could have been with a foster family free from the violence and substance abuse in my household, but I would be alone, away from my family and culture. And I already had enough of that experience at boarding school. She heard the horror stories about Navajo children being taken by social services and what they endured.

She opened her heart and home sparing me from all of that. To this day, my appreciation for my grandmother knows no bounds.

When my father was not drinking, he was very sharp and paid great attention to detail making sure he made an accurate diagnosis of any engine problem or fixing difficult mechanical problems on cars, trucks, and tractors. It was important for Father to properly troubleshoot everything and come up with an accurate solution. My grandmother would watch from the kitchen window as my father rummaged around in the engine like a surgeon, and she would smile.

*"Your father developed his love and passion for mechanical engine repair at a young age," she explained. "He would take apart the lawnmower and chainsaw just to understand the engine components and design. After taking apart the engines, your father would not know how to put them back together. But your grandfather never yelled. He just put the engines back together and went on with his day."*

Grandfather was also mechanically inclined and knew the basics of engine repair and welding. He was self-taught and knew the right questions to ask mechanics at the repair shops. Despite only an eighth-grade education, he could expertly read and understand vehicle repair manuals. To increase his reading fluency and comprehension, he would read the newspaper and magazines such as "Western Horseman".

My love of reading and wanting to understand as much as I can on subjects related to history, psychology, and societal experiences stems from my grandfather.

# CHAPTER 8

Making one's father proud is a quiet obsession. When I held my son for the first time, I had to smile at the irony. As children, we live to hear the words, *I'm proud of you.* Not understanding that those very same words would mean even more coming from my own two sons.

We lived and worked on my grandfather's farm, in the shadow of the Navajo Mine. My father, aunt, and a lot of other relatives worked at the Navajo Mine. Father worked as a heavy diesel mechanic making good money to support our family, but my relatives worked in various positions during different shifts because the mine was a twenty-four-hour operation.

Massive vehicles were something I became familiar with. Yellow dump trucks and front loaders filled the nearby lots and were lined up in rows. Dump trucks had a large bed to transport dirt and coal. A front loader had a large bucket in the front to hold dirt and coal when loading it onto a dump truck. Father repaired and serviced all of these.

Power generators with two large smokestacks for smoke to escape from burning coal were adjacent to the buildings. The smokestacks were one hundred stories high with small amounts of smoke coming out. At the time, those buildings seemed to tower over my small frame.

Navajo people played a pivotal role in ensuring and supporting the flow of electricity. People throughout the southwest depended on the Navajo Mine for their electrical needs. If the place shut down, people would not have power throughout the Western United States causing a major power deadlock.

Father often took me to his place of work when no one was home to take care of me. Rather than hiring a babysitter, my father had me tag along and hang out in his truck and the mechanic's shop. As long as I was quiet, nobody had a problem with my presence. One day, instead of walking towards the shop, we made our way towards the executive building where the all of bosses worked.

"We have to go inside and take care of some business," he said pausing at the door to give me a warning. "When we go inside, make sure you don't run around and be on your best behavior."

"All right dad, I'll be good. Why are we here?"

"You'll see, I have to meet with some people."

Inside the building was a metropolis of offices as far as I could see. We walked into the executive suite which had glass doors. Office workers, dressed in business casual attire, sat at their desks. The scent of coffee with the constant ringing of telephones filled the area.

After passing through the office area, we proceeded to the large board room. Father mentioned nothing about meeting his boss and other mining executives. As we entered, they were dressed in 1970s style business suits with butterfly collars, bell-bottom slacks, and large fat ties. The executives had greased hair with long sideburns much like the characters in the movie "The Godfather."

The boss stepped up to the podium. "Harrison, will you come to the front and receive your diploma."

Father straightened his yellow striped shirt and dark bell-bottom jeans before stepping forward.

"Congratulations Harrison, you have brought great credit to our organization. This diploma represents your knowledge and hard work. We appreciate everything you have done for our company."

As the room erupted into applause, I saw my father smile, and all of the pain and all the bad experiences vanished as I joined in and clapped for him.

"Thank you, sir." He shook the man's hand and walked towards me beaming with pride.

I had no idea that my father was even in school or that out of everyone in the family, he would choose me to witness his accomplishment. The way he buffed the frame with his shirt sleeve before handing the diploma to me.

You would have thought I was holding eternity in my hands. Maybe for some, it was just a Heavy-Duty Diesel Mechanic certificate, but I knew better. My father had many flaws. Some of his own making, and some that were beyond his control. For all that was wrong in our lives, this certificate was proof of what was right in our world. From that moment in time, he was the father I dreamt of; the man I wanted to emulate.

As I dropped my son off at college recently, I think back on that day. For every sleepless night where alcohol and screams hung heavy in the air, sometimes there was laughter. For every fight, there were times when my mother would be up late at night or early in the morning assisting him with interpreting the thick technical textbooks. Mother would have coffee made for my father so that he could study.

There was love there.

There *was* love there.

# CHAPTER 9

When I think of The Tó'aheedlíinii Lady taking that leap of faith into oblivion, her resolve always fascinated me. She had no idea where she was headed. Wherever it was, it had to be better than the edge of the cliff with the invaders baring down on her. For every silver lining, there is always a rumor of rain. For every good memory I have of my family, pain surely followed like thunder rolling in the distance. Children have this unwavering fountain of hope that even in the worst circumstances, the storms will blow over.

I thought that. My sisters thought that, but after a while love just isn't enough. The human psyche cries out for relief just as I'm sure my ancestors did when the invaders rode in from the direction of the sunrise. Being in an abusive relationship riddled with substance abuse is oppression like none other. When I turned seven, my mother had enough of domestic violence and alcoholism.

My mother and sisters showed up at my second-grade classroom in the Ruth N. Bond Elementary School located in Kirtland, New Mexico, which was named after a famous educator. Kirtland is in a high desert valley farm area along the San Juan River. Trees lined the front of the school which enclosed a large grassy lot located in the front of a white building constructed with bricks. The school had two major hallways which were connected by the front office.

Mrs. Stinson, the second-grade teacher, was at the front of the classroom explaining part of the English language. "All right class, pronouns describe the nouns to help make sentence structure a little easier."

A knock sounded on the thick, wooden door which interrupted her train of thought. "Class, finish writing your sentences while I answer the door." She came back with a concerned expression and gave me a gaze that shot through my soul. Somehow, I knew bad news was ahead.

"Darryl, come to the door. You have visitors," Mrs. Stinson announced.

Mother appeared scared as she glanced over her shoulder and then scanned the hallway in both directions, as though making sure no one was around. Mother always took care of herself making sure she was neatly dressed in matching make-up to impress any person. This time, she looked haggard and frail as she said, "Son, me, and your sisters are moving to Albuquerque. We have to get away from your father."

She had never said anything about her plans to leave him. Evidently, while he was away at work fixing heavy diesel equipment, she simply packed up my two sister's belongings and moved out. But what about me?

"Please do not tell your father or grandparents where we are going," Mother warned. "I don't want anyone to know our location. I'm afraid your father will find us,"

My young heart nearly stopped as I absorbed that shocking news. They were moving across the state to the largest city in New Mexico. My mother was taking her leap of faith and trusting that I would keep her secrets. Being asked to conceal the whereabouts of your mother and sisters was too much responsibility for a young child. This meant having to hold a poker face around my grandparents and father when they spoke of my mother.

Mother never explained why she was leaving so abruptly with no plans of bringing me with her. Abandoned children never understand why there are left behind. Perhaps my mother could not afford to take me? Some questions are best left unanswered.

"When will I see you again?"

Asking this question took every bit of strength in my body, spirit, and soul. I tried so hard not to break down and cry as a few tears rolled down my cheek. At that moment, everything within me felt so cold and empty, like a lost soul out of place.

"I don't know, son," she replied. "We have to find a home in Albuquerque. I will let you know when we have a place to live so that you can come with us. Take care of yourself, son," answered my mother.

My mother and sisters gave me a big hug and began walking down the long hallway. The school had a traditional setup with classrooms on both sides of the hall. After watching them, I returned to my classroom and had to play it off as though everything was all right.

My little sister ran into my classroom calling out, "Darryl!"

She grabbed me and would not let me go for what seemed an eternity. Slowly, she released me and rejoined my mother and older sister as they continued walking down the hall.

Some of the students in my class made fun of my sister. "Who is that little girl"? asked one student.

"She yelled after Darryl! Maybe she's his girlfriend," someone taunted.

In that instant, I understood how my father's anger flowed into his fists. Punching a few students would have brought immediate relief but little else. They had no clue what was going on. I heard what my mother said, and I even understood her decision, but she wasn't just leaving my father, she was leaving me.

After they left, the house was cold, dark, and empty as though the life had been sucked out of a living soul and left only a shell behind. The home that was once bustling with the noise of three children and some semblance of vibrant life, became as dead as dry leaves blowing in the wind.

When attempting to end an abusive relationship, the abuser may become more physically, emotionally, and financially abusive towards the victim to preserve the relationship. My father immediately cut off her insurance benefits and bank account access although they were still legally married. Mother had to overcome this fear of not having a financial cushion which took a considerable amount of courage.

My grandparents opened their home and kept me out of the foster care system despite the nature of my parents and their ill decisions. She became my guardian and enrolled me in a public school versus being sent back into that hideous boarding school. Needless to say, despite this better educational environment, my grades took a nosedive. My ability to concentrate on my schoolwork went out the door once my mother and sisters disappeared.

*I'm afraid Darryl is not keeping up with his schoolwork, the teacher said. His grades are not where they should be. He is not retaining the information I discussed in lessons. His needs may be best met in special education, they can help him in that class.*

Thank the Holy People and my ancestors for Grandmothers. Without missing a beat, my grandmother became my advocate and staunchest supporter. Whenever a parent-teacher conference was held, my grandmother was there fighting for me.

Grandmother sat down with me every night and went over school lessons. She took it upon herself to assist with my spelling and math. Without her intervention and advocating for me to receive services from a school psychologist, there's no telling where I would have ended up. With my grandmother and school psychologist's help, my grades improved and so did my outlook on life. She was an angel for providing me with the help and support I needed to survive and thrive.

In the early 1980s, there was no opposition to children being brought into a bar as their parents drank alcohol. My father took advantage of that. He provided me with money to play all the arcade video games that I wanted. Ten dollars was a lot for a child to blow on video games.

After one particular night of heavy drinking, my father took it upon himself to drive home. By this time, I was used to him getting behind the wheel under the influence. Close calls and near misses were commonplace for me as a passenger. The San Juan River is a major river in Northern New Mexico running through Farmington. As we were crossing the bridge over the San Juan River to get to Upper Fruitland, my father swerved his truck to the opposite side of the highway.

My life flashed before my eyes because we were going directly in the path of an oncoming car. My reflexes kicked in and I quickly grabbed the steering wheel and turned the truck back onto the correct side of the road. My father nearly drove off the road at least two more times before we finally made it home.

And just when things were looking up, my father checked out of my life, too. Father fell deeper into alcohol addiction which left me fending for myself. I no longer had a father in my corner to teach me the ropes of life. He handed over the insurance card to my grandmother and asked her to take care of me.

Father developed a relationship with Bella, whom he met at a bar. She was one of many women he brought home. Bella had older children given she was four years older than my father. For the most part, Bella was accepting of me and my father. She did her best to take care of my father by cooking for him, cleaning his laundry, and keeping our house clean. It was good to see my father happy and attempting to make a rebound. My father continued to drink heavily, whereas Bella stopped because she was carrying my half-sister.

Seeing my father being in a serious relationship with someone other than the home he once shared with my mother was bizarre, to say the least. He even seemed happy at the prospect of becoming a father again.

"Look son, you're going to be a big brother. This is the best birthday present," he said rubbing his girlfriend's stomach. Father had the biggest smile on his face and looked happy for the first time in a long while.

At first, I wasn't sure how to feel, but then the idea grew on me because I wouldn't be alone anymore. It was difficult to make sense of my new half-sibling and was not sure how to take it. Bella stopped drinking, and for a while there, we were one big happy family. Unfortunately, my father's addiction always seeped through the uneasy peace in our home.

Just like before, the alcohol flowed, and the party never stopped until someone was screaming and there was blood on the floor and the walls like the invaders closed ranks once more.

Bella stopped coming over after a while. My father beat her up, leaving her bloody with a black eye. His actions were unfortunate because Bella was a pretty lady and had a vested interest in my well-being. She was a good person since she had become sober and took the prenatal development of my new sister seriously. Since he wouldn't, or couldn't, join her in sobriety, she left him to his demons.

My father was stubborn and couldn't take direction and suggestions from any woman. Father wouldn't listen to my grandmother when she tried to correct him. He tried to quit drinking, but the addiction was too strong. The alcoholic spirit had a tight hold on father's soul and would not let go.

Once Bella left, my father took me to see a Navajo medicine man who was a guru healer in Navajo society.

A medicine man can communicate with deities and provide prayers and traditional chants to correct the manner. I give my father credit for trying to better himself and attempt to bring his family back together. Many attempts were made over the years. Father would be clean for a day or two, but then the walls would grow thin between his resolve and the addiction, and the cycle began again.

When my father was in one of his drunken stupors, I would always head outside to the strawberry bush my mother planted in her garden. It produced the sweetest strawberries in the spring. I watered it daily as a way of dealing with missing my mother and sisters. Sometimes there were more tears than water and my lingering thoughts.

*If the strawberries come back, maybe my mother and sisters will too.*

Painful words from a heart that still held out hope.

# CHAPTER 10

When The Tó'aheedlíinii Lady landed and took off in another direction away from her would-be captors, I wondered if she looked at the terrain beyond her ancestral home and thought, "What have I gotten myself into?"

When I finally had the chance to move to Albuquerque with my mother and sisters, I felt the same way.

Albuquerque is New Mexico's largest city located along the Rio Grande River in the center of the state. It was small compared to most metropolitan cities in the United States but is a big city for a kid from the Navajo Reservation. Grass was the only plant life present at local parks. Living there was a stark contrast to being at my grandparents' house. The place was a jungle with little vegetation and concrete covering most of the area.

The place was nothing like my grandparents' home where vegetation and livestock were everywhere. Back home, I was free to roam the endless expanse of my grandparents' farm and so much fresh air would fill my lungs. Living in Albuquerque brought feelings of entrapment like being caged and wanting to break free.

The urban environment is very different from living on the

reservation. A wide spectrum of people from different ethnicities and cultures live in what seemed, cramped areas and spaces. The attitude and diversity of people are what stand out the most. Life moves fast and it's reflective of people driving at high rates of speeds getting from one place to another which was a far cry from ambling along the dirt roads on the reservation.

In January of 1984, watering the strawberry plant paid off and I was standing on the edge of a cliff getting ready to take my leap of faith. I was leaving behind my father's addiction and my grandparents' love for what I hoped would be a better life in Albuquerque.

Leading up to the move, my mother was very affectionate and nurturing, but something was different. *She* was different. When I arrived, I was met with a surprise—my mother and sisters lived in stark poverty. My mother's path to acquiring a higher level of education meant we all had to struggle to make "ends meet". This meant living with limited food and other necessities.

Mother took her anger out on me. Her mentality shifted from one who nurtures to that of a provider and protector, but little else.

After waking up the first morning at my mother's apartment, she asked me to sweep the floor. My grandmother was my primary caretaker and she swept and mopped the floors when I lived with them. I quickly discovered that my best attempts were mediocre at best.

Mother angrily took the broom from my hand, "Give me that," she snarled. "Your grandmother did everything for you, but you have to sweep the floor like this—getting in the corners. If you leave crumbs, cockroaches and other bugs will come in!"

I wondered if she had been away so long that she'd forgotten me. My tasks were to care for the livestock and animals at my grandfather's discretion. Grandfather believed the man's responsibility was to do "outside" work.

"When I was with Grandmother—"

"This is *not* your grandmothers' house. Here, we have to conserve and use what we can," mother emphasized.

She had ceased being the nice mother and became a strict authoritarian figure.

When my mother went into her rage, my anger brewed. I thought about all I left behind to pursue an illusion of a happy family. As The Tó'aheedlíinii Lady picked her way through the canyon, I wondered if grief consumed her. Gone was her way of life and all she held dear. I imagined her crying until the world filled with her misery. I blinked away my tears and swallowed hard. Mother did not deserve the satisfaction of seeing me cry, so I kept my tears in. She had been getting mad by taking her frustrations out on me to deal with her stress. Perhaps she saw my father in me and scolding me gave her a chance to get back at him.

We had a small two-bedroom apartment; however, it was bare compared to my grandparents' house. The complex had three connecting apartments on each side with tan stucco walls, gravel, and small trees.

At that moment, the space bothered me a lot less than my mother's treatment of me. Soon, it felt as though I made the wrong choice agreeing to live with my mother and sisters. This move certainly did not produce the happy and secure feelings I longed for as I tended her strawberry bush back home.

"If you don't like it here, call your grandmother and have her pick you up," she taunted.

It was difficult to determine if she was serious or only trying to make a point. Immediately, my homesickness increased for my grandparents.

The ultimatum rang in my ears even after my mother made a desperate plea to have me live with her and my sisters. Her deception compared to the pattern I discovered again when I enlisted in the Army; a manner in which military recruiters painted a false perception of the military lifestyle to enlist recruits. Standing in the kitchen with my mother that day all those years ago reminded me of what the recruits receive as a "wake-up call" once they report to the in-processing station after swearing-in and signing their lives away.

My mother ceased to be the soft, quiet nurturing woman I longed for as she morphed into what amounted to a used cars saleswoman who sold me the forever lie. After her words, I eyed the phone on the wall.

The thought did occur to me to do exactly as she asked. After all, my grandmother always told me that when in need, to call her collect—a method of calling a person and they accept the charges on the opposite end.

I was a child torn between two families. My grandparents did not agree with my mother running away with another man because she was still legally married to my father. The mixed messages from my mother made me question ever wanting to live with her. The idea of returning to my beloved reservation where freedom was riding fast horses around the farm invaded my thoughts.

In retrospect, my mother had experienced a significant amount of trauma given she was beaten badly by my father. Post-traumatic stress does change the psyche and mentality of a person which increases anxiety. Growing up, my mother was a nurturing person, but her mentality had changed due to symptoms of post-traumatic stress.

In the early 1980s, the metropolitan environment was not conducive, encouraging, and supportive to young Indigenous women such as my mother. The world would not be fair for a young woman in my mother's financial situation. It took a considerable amount of strength for her to make the move to Albuquerque from the reservation to make a better life for herself. Despite my mother's poor parenting, she took it upon herself to start over while also acquiring an education from the University of New Mexico (UNM).

My mother was an undergraduate student and on a very fixed income. She was too proud to be on food stamps due to her mother's teachings about not relying on the government. Mother worked at the UNM financial aid office as a work-study student and was going to school full-time which meant long hours and very little food.

A half-pound of ground beef meat had to be used throughout the week for three to four different meals. The meat was mixed with spaghetti, macaroni with cheese, and potatoes. My mother bought chicken thighs and cooked them with macaroni in a crockpot. When we were out of meat, we survived on egg and bacon sandwiches.

This was very different from the abundance of food available at my grandparent's home. They always had a refrigerator full of food and being hungry was never an option. Grandmother canned fruits, vegetables, and homemade salsa. Processed beef from grandfather's cattle filled a large deep freezer.

The government had programs to help families in our situation, but my mother didn't want anything to do with it. Her belief was people should not depend on government assistance based on what my maternal grandmother taught her. Self-reliance was the battle cry for my mother, and she felt it better to not rely on any person or government program.

Street gangs and other unsavory characters populated our apartment complex. My mother did not allow us to leave the apartment compound for that reason. The neighbors were not always friendly, especially to Indigenous people. We were the first inhabitants of the land known as the United States but were still viewed and treated as second-class citizens; like the scum of earth and bottom of the food chain. I thought I had left all unhappiness behind, but living in Albuquerque was initially not a joyous occasion.

Perhaps my mother was under considerable stress from her classes and figuring out how she would pay the bills. "I am burning the candle at both ends" was a phrase typically used by my mother all the time. This meant she was doing everything possible to provide a safe roof over our heads. Sometimes, I took it to mean that life was wearing her down.

# CHAPTER 11

When I think of my mother and all the women of the Navajo Nation, I am reminded of The Tó'aheedlíinii Lady and her sacrifice and ultimate survival. I think of how women give up their dreams to follow love. Women are always changing, trying so hard to adapt to the newer surroundings. They are faced with impossible choices whether it's leaving an abusive relationship or leaving home to build a better life for themselves and their children.

Each requires a leap of faith and where The Tó'aheedlíinii Lady landed well, many do not. Sometimes they land hard or tumble deeper into the valley and the climb is further than they realize. That is the magic of women. They learn so much in the valley. Where men cut their way through, women glean. They pass through gathering what they can, learning whatever they can to advance to the next level. Women climb with children on their hips while challenges surrounding them like those invaders. Women, like The Lady, take that leap of faith and hope that the winds will also carry them to a safe place.

Mother put the rent at the forefront, otherwise, my family would be have been out on the streets. Luckily, we had a good relationship with the landlord who would allow mother to pay a little late. Sometimes, she would pawn her turquoise jewelry for extra income. We could survive with limited food and not have access to natural gas, but having a roof over our heads was much more important. Since we had an electric stove, in the winter, mother turned the oven on full blast to provide heat.

The 1980 Chevrolet Blazer she owned was prone to mechanical problems. So, when the car broke down, this meant the money typically used for the rent, utilities, and food went to auto repairs. This made it difficult for my family on a limited budget, especially since our food supply was deficient and this caused our utilities to be shut off.

The Blazer had to be properly maintained so mother could get to class and work. When it was in the shop, my mother had to take the city bus and walk to class. Overall, the family vehicle provided an important channel of money for my family.

We received most of our garments from the Navajo Nation which gave clothing and school supplies to enrolled members on an annual basis. In those days, the Navajo Nation gave two large bags of clothing including jeans, t-shirts, polo shirts, socks, underwear, shoes, and a jacket. Fortunately, the Navajo Nation helped us in this manner otherwise we would be dressed in old and torn clothing.

My mother, a trailblazer, set the standard for the entire family in what it meant to have goals and work toward achieving them. In addition to being a first generational college student, her first language was Navajo. She had to learn to comprehend and interpret the English language in an academic setting. Many Navajo students in my mother's situation struggled, but my mother persevered. She had to give extra effort to her classwork compared to her non-indigenous peers but managed to make friends with people from different cultures. She was always up late at night and awake in the early morning hours reading and studying those textbooks. Even on the days when she was dog-tired, she always pushed herself forever forward.

"Son, no matter what happens, you have to do your best in your classes. We may not have much in terms of monetary objects, but we have intellect and motivation and that counts for something," Mother emphasized.

As a first-generation college student, my older female cousins looked up to her as a role model. She filled an important role for fellow family members. Mother often provided technical information about financial aid and how to navigate the higher education system.

As a child, being at a flagship university broadened my mind and planted the idea of possibly going to college someday. Sometimes, we had to wait for my mother on the UNM main campus for her to finish work or classes.

Being on the campus was encouraging and enlightening because students were there to get their education. This invaluable experience fostered learning and education. Coming from the reservation with exposure only to Navajo people, walking around a large university was an eye-opening experience. Observing people studying and going to class, planted a seed in me to strive for better.

Whenever a Navajo student decides to pursue post-secondary education, the family also makes the sacrifice. Failure was not an option for her. Everything was on the line, and she was making a large investment. My mother had a lot of pressure to succeed.

As a family, we all sacrificed by not having expensive toys, the latest cassette tapes, and the ability to see the latest movies. We did not understand we were all sacrificing on my mother's behalf. As The Tó'aheedlíinii Lady had in riding into the wilderness and possibly to her death.

Mother depended on Navajo traditional prayers to help her navigate and succeed in her education. My maternal uncles were medicine men and would conduct prayer services for my mother and family. They found the value of education as being important and a catalyst for success. They prayed for us to be successful in our educational environment especially being in a metropolitan area. Living off the reservation meant that, in a sense, we were off-world and had to keep our wits about us. We clung to the old ways because we learned all too well how easy it was to get distracted, get lost, and go unnoticed in the classroom by the very teachers tasked to guide us.

# CHAPTER 12

What's in a name? A world, if you ask me.

The word "tribe" is a trendy term associated with a group of people that have a common interest fostering a positive sense of belonging. In my youth, to be identified and associated with a tribe was a degrading label considered a disgrace to society.

Stereotypes are often associated with Indigenous people. Being from the Navajo Tribe meant I was dirty, had drunk parents, and lived off welfare. To some sociology majors, we were a "burden to society" and we wouldn't amount to anything. Go back where you came from was an order meant for one race could easily be said for another. The late 1970s and early 1980s were not too far off from the 1960s and continued to carry racial undertones and civil unrest.

My new third-grade building had two adjacent classrooms in a separate location from the main school. The building had a dull gray, uninviting color that sent chills down my spine. After entering the classroom, with assistance from the school secretary, all eyes were on me.

"Follow me, I will take you to meet your new teacher," the secretary said as she walked me to my new classroom. She wore a long black dress matched with a white pearl necklace.

"You have a new student. He's from the northern part of the state. His name is Darryl and is new to Albuquerque," the secretary mentioned to my new third-grade teacher.

The woman, wearing a brown nylon blouse with large curly hair, glanced at me and asked,

"Darryl, where are you from?"

This was the first time hearing a New York accent which made me intrigued by how she spoke and made me also feel intimidated.

"I come from Upper Fruitland, New Mexico, which is near Farmington."

"Where is that? I am not too familiar with New Mexico," she asked.

"Upper Fruitland is located near the Four Corners."

The teacher took me to the front of the class, "Class, this is Darryl, he is from Upper Fruitland," my third-grade teacher announced. "Please help him get settled in."

Eyes peered at me, in the same manner, one would view a wild child. They took a pointed interest in my ethnicity. As we went back to her desk, she started peppering me with questions that made me feel like even more of an outsider.

*Who was your teacher at your previous school? How were your reading and math grades? Do you know the multiplication table? Does this spelling book look familiar?*

The first week was a honeymoon period, which brought me a certain level of comfort. However, it did not take long for the racial questions to pour in, but then my classmates had questions of their own.

*"Hey Darryl, do Indians still live in Teepees on the reservation?" A white student asked.*

*"Do Indians still do the rain dance? Is that why it rained today?"*

One Hispanic student announced to the class that he wrestled at a local club and would brag about his accomplishments. He was small in stature with brown hair and wore the latest 1980s styled clothing. However, he had an ego the size of the state. This student was the alpha male in the group and paid particular attention to me. He viewed me with curiosity and caution.

My cousin Vernon gave me a t-shirt with Airborne wings and a Ranger Tab. The alpha male student noticed my shirt and started making fun of me. "Look at him. He's wearing a shirt that says 'Ranger' on it. That's the only shirt he can afford," the student announced to the group.

"Look at him. Who wears a shirt with the word 'Ranger' on it?"

However, the alpha male clown did not understand the Airborne Rangers were an elite light infantry group in the Army which is a very difficult process to join. That clown did not know how hardcore Airborne Rangers are in the special operations community.

The more things changed, the more they stayed the same. I figured, since I left boarding school behind, surely things would get better. In a diverse setting, the teachers still did not pay attention to bullying which happened in the classroom and playground. Getting into physical fights with other students, just for being Navajo, seemed to be the norm.

The worst time was being jumped by four students as I walked home. Toby, the neighborhood bully, and his misfit crew lived on the next street and followed me home. They wore clothing associated with Cholo Mexican subculture of white t-shirts covered by flannel shirts buttoned to the top, baggy khaki pants, their hair was slicked back covered with a hairnet, and bandanas tied around their heads were pulled down to cover their eyes. Toby was a year older than me and ordered his three younger brothers to attack me.

"Surround and start hitting him," Toby ordered his brothers. The two thugs approached and started swinging haymaker punches. While dodging punches, I heard them whiz past my face.

"You better let them hit you or I will start to hit you myself," Toby ordered. And as Toby approached, it was best to take the beating from his two younger thug brothers. The other sibling was on standby in case I tried to run.

"Stay still so that I can hit you," a younger thug warned. As the adrenaline pumped through my body, it minimized their punches.

Blood ran from my nose after taking their blows. Crying and begging for mercy from the thugs never crossed my mind because they did not deserve the satisfaction.

They were nothing but a bunch of cowards and did not dare face me in a one-to-one challenge.

Toby ordered off the attack, "Let's go and let him bleed."

They laughed as they walked away. One of the brothers took my favorite hat. Now that made me upset.

After going inside our apartment and immediately locking the door, I cleaned myself up. Luckily, my sisters and mother were not home. Looking at myself in the mirror, the thought entered my mind, "Man, you can take a beating."

Bullies and gangs tend to attack in packs to give them a physical advantage. Similar to my days back in boarding school, most bullies were victims of some of the same kinds of harassment.

As The Tó'aheedlíinii Lady traversed the alien terrain of her time, I do not doubt that challenges pursued her like wolves nipping at her heels. But she was made of sterner stuff and looking at myself in the mirror, I smiled.

Maybe I was too.

# CHAPTER 13

One would think that I had gotten used to loud noises and people banging on doors. I didn't, but then who could prepare for Morris crashing into our lives? My mother had a married boyfriend whose family did not approve of her. And the feeling was mutual. The boyfriend was also censured by my father and family.

My mother met her married boyfriend in Nenahenzah, New Mexico. They maintained their relationship and were "living in sin" away from the reservation. Perhaps this is why she chose to move away from my father?

The best response in matters of the heart was no response. My position was even simpler: I permanently excused myself from the conversation. Other than living arrangements, I never questioned their relationship. Mother's adult affairs were none of my business and my only job was to be a child.

Morris was great for pounding on the door as I finished taking a shower, "Are you done?" he barked. "Come on, it has been five minutes!"

Disappointing Morris was not in my best interest especially given my history with my father. His voice was boisterous, probably from his Marine combat experience. However, this triggered my fight or flight response and overloaded my sensory perception. At that point, Morris' intention was difficult to understand. My experience with people being loud and direct often involved being hurt.

Morris was initially calm and collected. He appeared to observe my behavior and sized me up. He was tall in stature in comparison to my mother. Morris had long hair and wore it in a Navajo traditional bun wrapped with white yarn, tucked under a cowboy straw hat. Eventually, he felt the need to establish himself as the man of the house. Meaning, I would soon learn my place.

He was ten years older than my mother and had a wife and children. Given that Morris was a Marine in the Vietnam War, he was a strict disciplinarian.

"It should take you no more than five minutes to take a shower and be dressed," Morris growled.

Being showered, teeth brushed, and dressed in five minutes was a time crunch. Never a time to enjoy my showers which caused anxiety. To be rushed in that manner and treated as a Marine recruit going through Bootcamp. Maybe Morris was preparing me for adulthood through his strict discipline practices.

*Remember, you're only to take five minutes for a shower and get dressed. When I was going through Bootcamp, the drill instructors told us to be showered and ready in five minutes. Five minutes is all you get and all you need.*

Five minutes wasn't even enough to wash an ear!

Morris provided some financial assistance, doing what he could to help my mother. Although he presumably made good money being a Navajo politician, he also had the financial responsibility for his own family which means we came up short. Morris constantly returned to Window Rock, Arizona, when the Navajo Nation Council was in session. Once the session was over, Morris would check on his family in Nenahenzah. In this manner, Morris was living a double life being stretched financially thin.

Morris put a lot of miles on his truck with the constant traveling. Morris drove a 1970 Chevrolet Truck which was constantly breaking down. Then he would take the Trailways Bus to Gallup and his politician friends picked him up and transported him to Window Rock.

*With the money I have been using to support you and your mom, I could have a new truck now. I got this one on my first day out of the Marine Corps.*

My lasting impression of the man was that he always wanted to be the good guy. Oh, he did nice things for us, but there was always some hidden cost, some dig to remind us all that his benevolence was the only thing that stood between us and living on the street.

*Morris does not tell you 'no' when you ask him for things, make sure you do as he says.*

He was always quick to point out the Vietnam War Memorial of the three soldiers.

*Look at them. Of the three, are any of us represented in that statue? We Indigenous people proudly served in Vietnam without fear of the enemy. We lived and died for the American flag they buried us under and what thanks do we get? Forgotten that's what.*

There were days when the memories were close enough to sting. Morris discussed some of his Indigenous brothers he lost while serving overseas.

He did share his experiences going through Marine Infantry training at Camp Pendleton in California. Morris was medically discharged because a mortar round exploded near Morris, he survived but the blast killed fellow Marines in his platoon. He still had shrapnel in his legs. Morris received a Purple Heart for his gallantry having been wounded in combat.

Despite all of his war stories and successes, his family did not approve of the relationship he had with my mother. Whenever Morris' family had the chance, they attacked like a pack of wild animals with no empathy. Their only purpose was to create pain and chaos.

Baseball season in Albuquerque was a joyous time of celebration for my friends and family. At the end of the season, my baseball team typically had an after-season cookout.

After one celebration, the front door got kicked in by Morris' sons and his wife. They came rushing in like bandits going after their prey. She went after my mother, but she wasn't fast enough.

Mother struck that hideous woman in her head with a rotary phone. The wife had blood gushing from her head. My sister was grabbed by one of Morris' sons and the other son grabbed me. A strong kick to his leg caused him to loosen his grip allowing me to run to a neighbor's house for help. By the time the police arrived, Morris' wife and sons were gone. Not only did they traumatize us but stole items from our apartment.

Besides being cowards, they were the scum of the earth for stealing from poor people. But then again, they probably thought we were taking Morris away from them and we were not held in the best light either.

Either way, when my mother finally parted ways with him, I was able to take showers for as long as I desired.

# CHAPTER 14

*The journey across the desert was a long haul with little vegetation and water to survive on. The Tó'aheedlíinii Lady looked down at her once beautiful red dress and the threadbare places and frowned. She had worked so hard on the stitches and now some were frayed. Months had passed and while her food sources were scarce, a growth spurt made the garment snug in some places and baggy in others.*

*As one hour bled into another, whispers of her mother's ancestral home came to her that smelled of clay and spices. The grief-like scars still hummed with pain. Every step brought her out of the denied territory and closer to a place of rest. The Tó'aheedlíinii Lady took in a deep breath and almost wept in relief, as the sweet scent of vegetation and water kissed her soul.*

*Within less than a mile to go, the lapping sound of a water source sang to her, hastening her steps until she dropped to her knees and drank deeply from the spring. If anyone survived, by nightfall, hopefully she would be in the welcoming arms of her kinsman and they would wash away the soil and bathe her in the love she longed for.*

We were no different. With baseball season ending, a new excitement filled my soul. Leaving Albuquerque for the Navajo Reservation was more than an extended holiday. It offered the ability to return home. Baseball season was over, and it was time to enjoy being with my cousins.

Although reservations were meant to historically keep Indigenous people on a parcel of land, they provided "safe havens" from society in current times. Much of the land on the Navajo reservation remains inhabitable, either due to an isolated location or people choosing to live in the surrounding metropolitan areas. People choose to remain off the reservation even with all the amenities available in the city.

"Make sure you pack all of the clothes you may need for the summer," my mother warned while we scattered to our room to throw underwear and socks into bags. "When you're at your aunt's house, make sure you help out and be on your best behavior. I don't want to be having to come and pick you up."

My younger sister cried out, "What about my cat? Can I bring my cat?"

"Don't worry about the cat, just get your stuff together," I replied in my best "older brother so I'm the mature" tone.

My younger sister's response? She stuck out her tongue at me and took off running into the next room.

*So much for mature dialogue.*

No sooner had the thought entered my head, than it was overshadowed by the excitement that continued to build as we left the Albuquerque city limits. Summers on the reservation were always joyous occasions with my uncle, aunt, and cousins. Lukachukai was my mother's ancestorial home and it always filled my spirit with happiness and healing. Located on Navajo Route 12, about a two-hour drive north of Gallup, New Mexico, the Lukachukai mountains run along the Arizona and New Mexico border.

The community of Lukachukai is nestled on the west side of those mountains. Large red cliffs, look like huge pieces of rock pies that extend from the base of the mountain to the top. The base consists of red dirt with a mix of rocks with large pine trees filling the top of the mountain.

In the early morning, the sun creeps over the top of the mountain producing a light show of morning sunrays stretching across the horizon. A large natural creek runs from the top of the mountain separating my aunt's house from the base of the mountain. The water was potable in certain areas of the wash, given that the water is produced from natural springs on the mountain. The wash is a generic name for water streams in the Southwest.

When it rains or snows, people utilized four-wheel-drive vehicles for transportation. The roads get very muddy, and one needed to know how to drive in those hazardous conditions. People will park their vehicles off the highway and walk that mile just to get to their homes. In the winter, wood chopping is a necessity to ensure their homes are warm. Most homes do not have access to natural gas and propane is expensive.

Traveling to get groceries and other supplies, on average, is a two-hour drive. The Navajo Reservation is the size of the State of West Virginia in landmass but only contains nine grocery stores. On average, food prices are slightly higher than grocery stores off the reservation. Especially as it relates to fresh vegetables which are needed to gain a full spectrum of vitamins.

In my grandmother's generation, people tended to have a lot of children to help with the livestock and fields which was very different from the standard American nuclear family. My mother had eight siblings, three sisters, and five brothers. Growing up, my uncles, aunts, and cousins called me "Oscar" in reference to Oscar Meyer's brand of bologna, bacon, and hot dogs. Bologna and hotdogs were something I loved to eat, but I don't see why they needed to give me that name. I already had a name. That's family for you though. My cousins had nicknames for all of us and we never called each other by our real first names.

My maternal grandfather passed when she was young, so my mother, who was the second youngest of her siblings and was raised by her older siblings and my maternal grandmother. Grandmother raised all her children with most of my uncles becoming military veterans and medicine men. My other aunts, including my mother, became leaders in their respective fields. Leadership, education, and service to the country are trademarks of my family.

In stores, zucchini and cucumbers are transported from down south. Most times, those are loaded with fertilizer and preservatives. They were typically small and had a rubbery outside texture. However, given that fresh produce was expensive in stores and not always available, we grew our vegetables. Our zucchini and cucumbers grown on the reservation were bursting with water and had a wonderful taste from the earth and natural spring water utilized to grow our vegetables. Nothing beats the taste of zucchini and cucumbers right off the vine. The garden was two acres full of green chili, zucchini, yellow squash, tomatoes, and rows of corn. Adjacent to the garden, my aunt had a large alfalfa field.

During the late summer and fall harvest, we had so many vegetables that we preserved and gave away to relatives. We ate so much zucchini we had it coming out of our ears. We never tired of it, though. There were always traditional ceremonies that required a lot of food.

So, it felt good knowing the crops would go to good usage and would not be wasted. Some relatives came over asking for vegetables. My aunt could have easily charged them but felt it was better to give away the produce.

Waking up early was a practice learned from my late paternal grandfather. According to Grandfather, the sun was not supposed to see you sleep otherwise the daily blessing would be given to someone else. Additionally, it was encouraged to run or do some type of strenuous activity to build stamina and make your mind strong.

"Oscar, are you ready to turn the water on?" My cousin Vernon asked. We called him "Boss".

He was seven years my elder and kept us all in line. Every day like clockwork he'd nudge me and ask, "Wash your face and brush your teeth. We have work to do!"

I was barely out of the bathroom before he'd urged me through the kitchen and out the door.

Each day, my responsibility was to turn the irrigation water on at the source. Waking up at the crack of dawn to walk along with the wash for a mile upstream to shift the spring water to my aunt's vegetable garden was a daunting task. Being an early riser, my cousins tended to depend on me to turn the irrigation water from the natural spring wash to provide much-needed moisture for the garden and alfalfa. The reward for waking up early and walking along the stream was the sweet smell of the vegetation and the water.

In the southwest, the environment is typically arid but the vegetation along the wash was a natural oasis in the desert. The area around the wash was full of natural grass along with trees providing a green landscape in a rocky environment. Water spiders grazed the surface as though they owned the water.

Turning the water on meant diverting water from the local spring into the irrigation system. At the mouth of the irrigation ditch, dirt had to be placed to serve as a mini dike diverting water into an irrigation ditch leading to my aunt's vegetable field. The rest of the wash water was preserved for other farmers to use downstream making sure we were considerate and mindful of our neighbors.

Next, the water had to be followed as it flowed down the ditch smoothing out rough edges with the shovel. Any debris which may block the easy flow of water was removed. This took a lot of responsibility and knowledge of irrigating fields.

"You should not depend on Oscar so much to make sure the water is adjusted," Aunt May mentioned to my cousin. The thought occurred my ability to take care of the task was without any worry or concern. Besides, it got me out of the house and made me feel useful.

"I don't have to worry about him because he has experience irrigating for his grandpa in Upper Fruitland," Vernon said to Aunt May.

"But still, you need to check the ditch and make sure there is no leaking water. We cannot waste the water coming from the mountain. Oscar may have some trouble fixing the ditch by himself."

My aunt was right, if the dirt ditch broke open, my arms did not have enough strength to fix a major breakage. If a significant amount of water was lost, it would not be good for the crops. In the back of my mind, I knew my cousin was using me to do his work. Aunt May set my cousin straight, but then that was always her way. Looking out for the little guy was a way of life for her. I know my small arms were grateful for it, but I have to admit, after hearing the conversation, I didn't feel like a 'little guy." The fact that my older cousin had faith in my abilities made me feel ten feet tall which was pretty big for a ten-year-old.

As the matriarch, Aunt May had clan rights to the land and water resources. She was our leader and hero and treated all of us with care and love which can never be replicated. No other lady had more love for her children, grandchildren, nieces, and nephews. Aunt May always drilled home the idea of acquiring a college degree and that we were just as competitive as anyone from whichever background and culture.

She always emphasized the importance of preserving water because, as it was then and how it is now, water is scarce and sacred on the Navajo reservation. Water is the source of life, and every part of nature depends on it. Aunt May allowed us to play in the wash, but always encouraged us to not waste the potable water. A lot of our other distant relatives did not have running water and electricity. Often, we volunteered to haul potable water for our relatives who lived away from the wash.

Water had to be pumped with a metal handpump which was a good workout. The older cousins were a lot bigger than me and could easily handle the task. When filling large, galvanized metal containers, we often traded off as we pumped ensuring someone with rested muscles was always pumping the water. This made for a quicker process and allowed us to rest. The well water had a sweet taste and was always cold given it was embedded in the ground.

Tó'aheedlíinii, which I stated earlier, is translated as Water Flows Together, is the clan of my mother and late Aunt May. The Navajo people are a matrilineal and matrilocal society, with each person belonging to four different clans. The first clan is from the mother, the second is the father, the third is the maternal grandmother and the fourth is the paternal grandfather. Women are the leaders and had the upper hand in decisions as it relates to the land, livestock, and the well-being of the family.

Since my aunt and my mother were full sisters, she was also my mother in our clan. All my cousins, including myself, had the utmost respect for her because she was our matriarch.

*Our clan emerged from two creeks that fed both of our villages. When our population swelled beyond our borders, we migrated to Lukachukai and other areas in Arizona.*

Aunt May would recount our history before telling us of her time attending Sherman Indian boarding school in Riverside, California.

*I found love there. I met your Uncle Leonard there. We weren't rich to some, but I look at all of you and laugh. We're rich in love and that's just about the same.*

Growing up, my aunt and uncle never spoke negatively about their boarding school experience. They emphasized that education is important, and the ancestors paid for our opportunity to be in school. Once we acquired our education, we would make use of it and help the people.

Waking up early was second nature. It was best because the weather became warm in the summers on the reservation. Tough labor work was best performed in the morning versus dealing with the hot sun.

In the Navajo language, permission had to be asked from the water spirit in the form of a prayer to utilize the water. This concept was taught by my late grandfather who offered corn pollen for the nourishment of our crops

"Hold on, let's take the truck so we can go shoot around later," Vernon said with a mad twinkle in his eye. Vernon always carried a thirty-thirty rifle. This round was effective for taking out crows and patrolling the vegetable and alfalfa fields to protect the crops from the crows and other small animals.

I idolized my cousin Vernon. That Fall, was Vernon's senior year in high school. We all respected and looked to him because he was attending Farmington High, ran on the track and field team, was a silversmith, and planned to enlist in the Army. Serving in the military, despite the racial undertones we faced in society, was a family tradition. A lot of us menfolk from the Tó'aheedlíinii clan, including myself, became paratroopers in the military.

On this one morning, Vernon drove us to the base of the wash to turn on the water, he had a light brown small Isuzu pick-up truck with an orange stripe that ran down the middle which was popular in 1985. Living in this era meant no cell phones, internet, and Apple radio. Our method of recording music was waiting for the songs to play over the radio, then recording them. That year, Vernon had a haircut that mimicked Marty McFly like the movie, "Back to the Future."

My aunt and uncle had recently bought Vernon a truck because he went to high school in Farmington, New Mexico, and my other cousin, Leon, wrestled on the varsity team at Shiprock High School. Leon, a year younger than Vernon, also served as a role model and spent his high school summers in California working as a plumber journeyman. When Leon came home, he was typically loaded with cash and bought us whatever we wanted since he worked as a plumber.

Vernon installed a cassette deck along with making specialized boxes for customized six-by-nine speakers. As a silversmith, Vernon was creative and knew how to design speaker boxes. He made simple jewelry and specialized in silver scorpion pins made of turquoise. Since Vernon attended Farmington High, their mascot was a scorpion and Vernon made extra money selling the scorpion pins to his peers.

Growing up, we didn't have expensive toys. Vernon would make model guns out of two by four wooden boards and plyboards utilizing his intuition and creativity to make them resemble real machine guns. Although they were not paint guns, they still allowed us to patrol while believing we were shooting paint rounds. We typically drove in Vernon's truck and picked up other relatives and friends to assist in our war games.

Night Ranger's song "Still Rock in America" became the soundtrack for that particular summer as we made our way to turn the irrigation water on. Vernon and my other cousins enjoyed rock music at the time and often played their cassette tapes so much until the tape itself snapped.

Since traveling to Farmington or Gallup was at least a two-hour drive, we became experts at repairing broken tapes. There was something euphoric about owning a cassette tape and taking out the cover and reading the lyrics and credits. In some way, this increased our reading fluency and comprehension by trying to understand the meanings of the songs.

Along with baseball and times at my grandparents' home, these are also some of the happiest memories.

# CHAPTER 15

*The Tó'aheedlíinii Lady settled by the lake, enjoying the way the sunlight shimmered on the water like a promise of good tidings. She sobbed with relief as the water soaked into her moccasins and soothed her feet. After a while, a smile tugged at the corners of her lips as the gentle nudge of a fish caught her attention. Her stomach grumbled in protest as she leaned back against the stones.*

*The Tó'aheedlíinii Lady quickly swept up a fish and tossed it on the shore next to her.*

*The future is patient. I shall take care of this wrinkle in the belly for the moment.*

*She'd come a long way, but there was still so much further to go.*

Irrigating the fields in the morning kept the water from vaporizing in the hot sun. When the irrigation water seeped into the ground, earthworms would emerge to greet the morning sun. Earthworms provided oxygen to the ground by making small pathways to the soil and served as bait for trout fishing. As we irrigated, earthworms were collected for our afternoon fishing affairs at the lake. The cool breezes which came across the lake provided relief from the brutal heat of the Arizona sun.

Vernon asked, "Wanna go fishing later?"

"All right, I can sure use a day of fishing," I replied.

My cousins only had two fishing rods, which presented a small problem. We had limited money acquired by selling alfalfa hay and helping at the Catholic Church. Purchasing Navajo Nation fishing licenses was not in our budget. So we utilized soda cans and attached the fishing line along with the hooks and weight at the end.

Rainbow trout and catfish were caught with a technique of wrapping the fishing line with the aluminum can. A standard fishing rig was rotated by the flinging of the wrist and launched with centripetal force. This required a lot of practice to perfect. Whenever the Navajo Rangers from the Navajo Nation Park and Recreation Department showed up, we simply released the cans into the lake. We'd retrieved them once the Rangers left.

We often fished at Tsaile Lake, which is one of the larger manmade lakes utilizing a flood-controlled dam at the head of Canyon Del Muerto. The community of Tsaile is in a majestic valley surrounded by pine and cedar trees. Lukachukai Mountain was a beautiful backdrop to Tsaile Lake.

A local stream provided fresh water to the lake. Navajo Nation Fish and Wildlife often stocked the lake with rainbow trout and catfish. The Tsaile Lake is adjacent to Dine' College at the intersection of Navajo Route 7 and Route 12, about a two-hour drive north of Gallup, New Mexico. People from throughout the reservation and border towns come to Tsaile to camp and fish.

"Oscar, did you just have a bite on your line?" Vernon asked.

"I may have, because I felt a tug."

"We'll stay here until we catch a few more fish then." Suddenly, his demeanor changed. "Oscar, I think a Ranger's coming. Let go of your line, he's coming around the hill."

A chill came up my spine noticing the Ranger's vehicle approaching. A large fine and confiscation of fishing equipment would happen if we were caught without a fishing license. Five dollars was all that was in my wallet, and I couldn't afford the hefty fine. Having only a soda can with a fishing line and rig, the Rangers wouldn't confiscate much from me. The thought crossed my mind of being hauled off to jail for illegally fishing.

"Just be cool Oscar, everything will be all right," Vernon assured me as he reeled in his fishing line and placed his rod by his side. Vernon did his best to remain calm, understanding his persona provided confidence to the rest of us.

The Ranger pulled up in a white four-by-four Chevrolet Pick-Up with a large star emblem on the door, a spotlight on the driver's side, and a red and blue light on the cab like a police vehicle. As the Ranger passed, he gave a simple wave of his hand noticing our presence and went about his business.

He rolled down his window. "You guys catch any fish?" The ranger asked as he scanned our fishing camp with a radar gaze searching for anything that was against the rules.

"Naw, we've been here all morning and we only got a few bites," Vernon said.

"What about you? Are you fishing?" the ranger asked me.

"I'm just here to observe and hang out." The ranger had an expression, probably thinking it was odd for me to not be fishing. He crossed his arm and looked me up and down, evidently getting a visual verification that I was telling the truth.

Finally, the ranger uncrossed his arms and presented with a more relaxed and calmer look. "You're missing out if you ain't fishing. This part of the lake is known to have lots of fish."

The ranger put his truck in gear and slowly started driving off. "You guys take care and I'll see you around."

The adrenaline left my body thinking to myself, *What a close call!*

"It looks like the Ranger is leaving. Get your can and bring in your line," Vernon ordered. "I'm sure your bait is gone from your line,"

We often used worms, bugs, and corn for bait. Worms and bugs were preferred over corn knowing fish would have difficulty digesting it, and we had to be responsible for the well-being of the fish.

"All right Oscar, rebait your line and toss it back out," Vernon instructed.

After pulling my fishing line in, and putting more corn on the hook, the baited fishing rig was twirled in a circular motion allowing centrifugal force to launch it in the air. Corn was flying in all directions.

"Oscar, go easy on your cast otherwise you'll lose the bait," Vernon warned.

Parts of Tsaile Lake dropped off to thirty feet not far from the shore. I intended to get my fishing rig in the deep part of the lake knowing fish tended to skim the bottom. Although I was fishing with a can, I wanted to catch a bigger trout than my cousins who were using fishing rods.

"All right, I'll take it easy on my casting," I assured him.

My cousin was right, we could not waste our bait because we only had one can of corn and ten earthworms we found in the garden. The fish we were catching was going to be our dinner given we did not have much food in the refrigerator at my aunt's house. The menu tonight was going to be fresh rainbow trout with zucchini and corn from the garden. My mouth was already watering. Hence, we couldn't wait to get home.

Once the fish were caught, we immediately gutted and placed them into a cooler. We typically threw small fish back into the lake so they could have a chance to grow larger. When we arrived at my Aunt May's house, we either cooked the fish or put them in the freezer for later consumption. We always consumed what we caught, and it was never wasted. One of our cousins from California came to visit and for some reason, he left his catch on the ground.

Aunt May observed this incident and stressed to us, "We are not to be fishing, only to be leaving the fish to rot." She always encouraged us to have respect for animals and all of nature. Then to Vernon, she said, "Make sure your cousin knows that we don't waste the fish."

When the other cousin was approached, he flipped back, saying, "Yeah, I was going to clean the fish."

However, the fish was not in a cold environment to preserve its meat. It angered me knowing we could have eaten the fish enjoying its fresh taste.

On the reservation, we had plenty to keep ourselves occupied. Besides fishing, we also hiked up and down the Lukachukai mountain. My family had a cabin at the base of the mountain which served as a summer home. Often, we spent our evenings at the cabin enjoying the beauty around us that extended to the tall pine trees and thick oak trees. But for all of the healing spaces I encountered on the mountain, part of me felt the whistling absence of my father in my life.

My cousins did the best they could to fill in the gaps and I love them for it, but there were times when I wanted to connect and talk with my father about life and the mysteries therein. The day my cousin handed me my first Playboy magazine, I had questions, millions of questions.

"What do you think of Miss June?" Vernon teased.

Looking at naked women at that age was too much for me to process. "She has big boobs," I managed, not sure whether that was the right or wrong response.

Having older cousins meant having access to some thought-provoking information which was mind-blowing. As I looked at the pages, I wondered how someone could be naked in a magazine.

*"I am both a mother and father to you."*

I remember my mother saying those words often when I was growing up. Financially, she was the breadwinner in our household. As such, she had to think for two parents instead of one. As an adult, I understood what she was attempting to say, but to this day, this idea of my mother considering herself my mother and father still does not resonate with me. Some things required a man's guidance.

Despite our complicated relationship, I *needed* my father. Young men need their fathers or prominent male role models to teach them the mechanics of hunting, fishing, and being a warrior.

When it comes to indigenous hunting and fishing, a skill is typically passed down from a father, uncle, or grandparent. The same could be said for sex education. Young men may feel more comfortable asking their fathers or other male role models. I certainly did.

Growing up with my cousins and uncles provided those 'man talk' conversations that I expected to have with my father. Receiving sex education "rez style" from my cousins was memorable at best especially when they were trying to navigate those choppy waters themselves. But they were there for me, my cousins and uncles, sharing laughter, love, and all the good memories in between.

# CHAPTER 16

*The rains have come and gone and the Sage sings to the muds and the night air. When you are older, I will show you how we use this plant in our ceremonies, for now just know the Sagebrush is plentiful here in Lukachukai and the medicinal scent will refresh your spirit.*

*The Tó'aheedlíinii Lady abandoned her pallet to walk while the questions were hanging heavy in her spirit. The seasons had been kind to her in her mother's ancestral home. Loneliness poked at a raw place in her as the talks she longed to have with her mother ached in her throat.*

*Had there been more time, she was sure her mother and the other women in the village would have educated her more on the ways of women. Instead, her mother's people prepared her, but the questions lingered, and the grief returned, filling her eyes with tears and heart with memories of all that was lost. She ran a hand over her stomach and took in a deep breath.*

*All that you ask is yours, my child, until the sun and the moon become one.*

Later, though I never questioned my mother about this part of her life, I did find out that my mother and I had more in common than I thought. My experiences at boarding school paled in comparison with what she endured.

As a girl, my mother attended the Lukachukai Boarding School. She would walk along the Sagebrush to get to and from the small building miles from her home.

Mother, along with my uncles and aunts, attended the boarding school which was run by the BIA. The Bureau of Indian Affairs (BIA) which later transitioned to the Bureau of Indian Education (BIE) initiated boarding schools to assimilate children into everyday society by forcibly removing them from their homes.

After being removed, their long hair was chopped off, heads were shaved, and the children were forced to conform to Eurocentric values. Even back then, extreme discipline practices were used to cancel out Indigenous language and culture.

Additionally, Indigenous children were converted to Christianity and instructed in a military type of environment and they had to wear Eurocentric-based school uniforms. Language and culture were whitewashed out of children by being subjected to harsh punishment for simply speaking their language and practicing their customs.

She indicated she made meaningful relationships there despite the harsh discipline methods. She made a lot of friends and relations with people throughout the community. She never identified herself as a "boarding school survivor" or talked negatively about her experience, but the signs were there, sometimes in her look or the way she pushed herself to succeed.

Mother and her generation were tough people and defined the epitome of resiliency. My late maternal grandmother stressed the importance of acquiring college degrees and certificates to become successful. Although boarding school was much rougher back in my mother's generation, she endured the hideous and demoralizing setting to do what was best for her future family.

Grandmother, and other relatives, were visionaries and could see the future. Before World War Two, Navajo elders were able to visualize a large-scale war on the horizon although they did not speak and comprehend the English language. Somehow, they analyzed the rapid change in the environment which forewarned them about the upcoming war. World War II.

The elders were able to metaphysically input information using prayer, meditation, and traditional songs. When medicine men or women conduct a traditional ceremony, they typically had visions providing insight and guidance from the Holy People. In this manner, the Holy People informed the medicine people about current and future events which may be detrimental to the Navajo people.

Grandmother prepared my mother and aunts for boarding school by bringing them into the traditional sweat lodge. A traditional Navajo sweat lodge was a small dome structure put together with small logs and reinforced with dirt. Lava rocks are heated in a large fire bringing them to a red glow. The hot rocks are brought into the lodge, making the temperature increase which is uncomfortable to bear.

My uncles went into the male sweat lodge to prepare their minds for the rigors of learning and surviving western education. Resiliency, in the traditional practices, was needed for people enduring the boarding school experience. The human mind and psyche could be strengthened by the heat of the sweat lodge.

The recent discovery of the bodies of Indigenous children who once lived in residential and boarding schools has brought past trauma and negative memories into current consciousness. This has reopened old wounds of people who have repressed their feelings associated with their time there. Some have reacted by burning Catholic churches in a passive-aggressive manner. Indigenous people are upset and are not backing down because some churches which were burnt down were over 100 years old.

While my mother never spoke about it openly, it was well known that some of my relatives were sexually abused by church officials. Catholic priests and other important people of power were able to escape persecution. Frustrated by justice denied, some of the Navajo people lashed out instead of reasoning together, and finding nonviolent ways to heal what was broken.

Despite the mistreatment of my people, the Catholic Church emerged and converted Indigenous people to Catholicism. As a child, my mother made me take catechism classes given the fact that the Catholic Church had a large influence on the reservation. As children, we did what we could to help the Catholic Church in Lukachukai called St. Isabelle's Church.

Even with the historical atrocities of the Catholic Church, we seemed to have pleasant relations with the church. For many of us, we viewed the church as a social interaction center. My cousins sponsored dances at the Catholic Church Hall with makeshift disc jockey equipment. They also put together a disco ball with broken pieces of mirrors.

My cousin Vernon was the disc jockey and he played music from the popular artists of our day including Michael Jackson, Bryan Adams, The Cars, Journey, and music from the movie "Footloose."

We did our best to mimic and copy the movie "Footloose" with the lights and glitter on the floor. Decorating for church dances was an all-day affair and any money we raised went directly to the Catholic Church. It was innocent fun. I mean there we were, jockeying for position in the mirror as we took forever trying to make our hair the same style as our favorite stars.

And with a storm of glitter and music not our own, embracing a culture that was not entirely our own—was complete.

# CHAPTER 17

*Many years had passed since that fateful day when the enemy tribe had attacked. The rain provided much-needed moisture to medicinal plants, tobacco, and herbs The Tó'aheedlíinii Lady needed for the traditional ceremonies. Her son walked toward her with his younger sister trailing behind him. She smiled at the leaves peeking from the girl's chubby hands cupped to her stomach.*

*Why do we search for these things, Mother?*

*The Tó'aheedlíinii Lady looked out on the expanse of trees beyond the children and frowned*

*One day, many will be forced to leave this place. Some will never come home. Some will be hidden in the hills. It is for them we gather. For them, we shall sing them home.*

Navajo people still utilize traditional medicine for health, wellness, and spiritual purposes.

My family always had traditional ceremonies conducted for various family members. This often required a great deal of assistance from relatives in terms of labor, food, gathering of traditional supplies, monetary goods, and money to pay the Medicine Man or Woman. The

Medicine Man or Woman is very similar to a guru or priest in that they know the methodology and process of Navajo ceremonies.

Sometimes, we had to drive halfway across the reservation to pick up the Medicine Man or Woman. While the ceremony was being conducted, we often had to collect herbs and other materials requested by the Medicine Man or Woman.

Other times, we collected firewood for cooking and heating. Trees weren't chopped down for monetary gain, they always had an important purpose. Navajo traditional ceremonies required a lot of firewood. Fortunately, we were able to gather wood with a permit from the chapter house.

In the 1980s, my Aunt May and Uncle Leonard would invite different medicine men to conduct ceremonies. Some of the Medicine Men were in their 80s which meant they were born at the turn of the century. One medicine man, in particular, mentioned his grandparents were on the Navajo Long Walk from the Navajo Reservation to Bosque Redondo in present-day Fort Sumner, New Mexico, which took place between 1863 and 1866.

During this forced march, much like the Trail of Tears, 10,000 Navajo people walked over 250 to 400 plus miles. Many were shot on sight by the cavalry for not keeping up with the forced march. Once Navajo people reached their destination, they were interned at Bosque Redondo, New Mexico, where many died due to horrible living conditions. The soil was too alkaline to grow vegetables and the Navajo were unable to hunt wildlife.

Rations of bleached flour, salt-preserved bacon, and other preserved commodities were issued to Navajo people. Once our people were exposed to preserved and bleached food, they developed diabetes and other inhibiting health problems. The soldiers showed no mercy for women, children, or families. The Navajo people became prisoners of those with the intention of assimilation and annihilation.

Deep into the night, the Medicine man spoke of the trials and tribulations our ancestors endured and the lessons we needed to learn from their songs and stories of survival.

*My grandparents were at Bosque Redondo and survived. Some of these songs we are going to sing in this ceremony were devised when they were held in captivity. They said we must hold on to our traditional ways and ceremonies. They told me a lot of important medicine people died over there.*

As the Medicine Man started singing the traditional prayer songs, the entire group gathered. That evening, the Hogan, which is a Navajo traditional home in the shape of an octagon with a chimney and a single door to the east, started humming. And I got the sense that the ancestors were singing and helping us to remember each song or story. A feeling washed over me and beyond a shadow of a doubt, I knew the Medicine Man was right. For our people to survive, we needed to hold onto our traditional ways to be strong.

Historically, the Navajo people were released from captivity once they signed the Treaty of 1868. According to the Medicine Man who joined us that evening, the captured people utilized traditional methods to gain a tactical advantage in negotiating that treaty. The Treaty indicated that the Navajo people were no longer going to commit acts of war against the United States.

Navajo people were confined to a particular reservation that had boundaries with home allotments for grazing livestock and home placement. The development of a medical care delivery system and the initiation of Western Eurocentric education on the Navajo reservation were both discussed and negotiated. This was the overall inception of having boarding schools on the Navajo reservation.

As we sat in the ceremony late into the night, the Medicine Man provided additional education.

*My relatives, we cannot forget what our people have endured to bring us what we have today. This ceremony I am conducting, do not take it for granted. Learn about the ceremony and keep it going for our children.*

*The next set of songs we are going to sing was devised when the people returned from Bosque Redondo. When they saw Tsoodził (Mount Taylor near Grants, New Mexico), they were overfilled with joy and sang songs that were associated with the occasion.*

Once the Medicine Man sang the songs associated with Navajo returning home, the entire Hogan began to resonate and hum. It appeared the ancestors and Holy People were singing with us. The love and joy were felt in my heart realizing we are a strong and resilient people.

Navajo people were buried at Bosque Redondo, so the Navajo people are empathic and have a collective unconscious about having their relatives buried at a different location. To this day, the relatives are still buried there and never came home.

In comparison to the Navajo people, other Indigenous groups were not as fortunate to preserve their languages and culture. Over time, Indigenous people will learn to heal from episodes of post-traumatic stress disorder they are experiencing from boarding or residential schools. Indigenous people can heal with their faith and support from family.

# CHAPTER 18



*The Tó'aheedlíinii Lady smiled as her grandchildren prattled on circling the area where she rested. She caught her son staring at her and reached for his hand.*

*If they are bothering you, I can send them inside.*

*With a shake of her head, she patted his arm. "Children are built to play. The old are built to remember."*

Navajo people did not become United States citizens until June 24, 1924. This is not very long ago in comparison to other races and ethnicities in the United States. My grandfather was a kindhearted man who never displayed symptoms of post-traumatic stress.

Although my grandfather was forced to learn English and only attended school up to the eighth grade, he volunteered to become a Navajo Code Talker. Despite all the social injustice and racial prejudice, my grandfather chose to serve his country. As Indigenous people, we are the highest per capita in comparison to other races, to serve in the military.

My grandfather, along with a lot of Indigenous people serving in World War II, served their country proudly. However, when Grandfather was born, he was not a citizen of the U.S. After he was discharged, he was not allowed to vote because he lived on the Navajo reservation.

*When I came home from the war, I found a job in California and started working around Upper Fruitland; they would not let me vote. I fought for this country, almost died for this country and still, they refused me that right.*

Before my grandfather passed, my service in the Army was spent in the 75th Ranger Regiment which is an elite light infantry unit with a high level of difficulty to enter. Being Airborne means you are a special breed. Our unit was not for the faint of heart. Jumping out of an airplane may be insanity to others. However, Airborne was thought of as a joyride for us. Something I'm sure The Tó'aheedlíinii Lady world heartily endorses. She carved the path and made it easy for the menfolk from the Tó'aheedlíinii clan to continue in her tradition.

Saint Michael is the Patron saint for Airborne personnel for protection and guidance in times of war. As a Navajo from the Tó'aheedlíinii clan, The Tó'aheedlíinii Lady provided me with guidance, protection, and insight. Fortunately, stories have been told and preserved about my clan. In dark times, these stories give me hope and strength to carry on no matter how difficult the journey may be. We cannot ever give up because our ancestors give us the power to overcome any obstacle and barriers.

Grandfather told me a story about when his company helped a pinned down Army Airborne unit in the South Pacific. The unit made a jump but were cut off and trapped from any reinforcements. To prevent their total annihilation, grandfather and his company of Marines fought off the Japanese and were able to save the airborne unit.

Before this, grandfather did not know anything about paratroopers and was amazed they could jump out of an airplane and hit the ground running.

When my grandfather was told about my involvement in an Airborne unit, he had a lot of questions about how parachutes worked and how it felt to jump out of an aircraft filled with military equipment.

*We found parachutes on the beachfront and wondered how they worked and operated. I made friends with some of the paratroopers. At the time, I did not want to ask too many questions out of respect for them. The paratroopers carried carbine rifles with a metal folding stock. They had M1A1 Carbine rifles and were able to fold but extend for better accuracy. We carried the M1 Garand with a solid wooden rifle stock.*

I still remember the day I told him that I was with an Airborne unit. The mixture of pride and disbelief warmed my insides; especially when he asked what it was like to jump out of an airplane.

I told him, *it is crazy to jump out of airplanes with all of that equipment. Once I'm out there with the wind rushing past my face while tumbling toward earth, there's no way to describe it. I mean it was fun, but there's this overwhelming sense of freedom. It's hard on the knees and the back though.*

I loved sharing those experiences with my grandfather. The stories seemed to take him out of himself as his health declined. He was battling diabetes at the time. Grandfather was delighted to hear about how parachutes are packed and deployed in the air, and how it felt to exit the aircraft and hit the ground.

Although my grandfather's health was declining, my relationship with him went on a deeper level. Perhaps that was why he felt comfortable explaining his role in World War II. After my grandfather passed, my deepest appreciation for that time was finally hearing about his experiences.

Kenji Kawano, a well-known author, is married to a Navajo and wrote a book about the Navajo Code Talkers. In the process of writing, Kenji drove to different parts of the Navajo reservation and interviewed living Code Talkers in the early 1990s.

One morning, we were outside of my grandparents' home doing our ranch chores when out of the corner of my eye, a small Japanese manufactured car slowly crept down the driveway. A tall slender Japanese man exited the car with a clipboard and camera.

He asked, "Excuse me, is this the home of Harrison Lee Benally?"

We replied, "Yes, you're at the right location." Grandfather was informed Kenji was there to see him.

"Who is that guy?" Grandfather asked giving the man a once over.

I knew the man was in town asking questions about the elders that served as Code Talkers, but I was hoping that he would skip our home because my grandfather had been so reluctant to talk about his past.

"Kenji is here to ask you about being a Code Talker."

Grandfather was wearing his work clothes and had grease on his shirt from working on his tractor and didn't seem intimidated. "How does he know I was a Code Talker?"

Kenji presented as a friendly guy wearing a polo shirt and shorts with cargo pockets. He looked like a tourist with an expensive camera strapped around his neck.

Our guest extended his hand to my grandfather and asked, "Are you Harrison Lee Benally and did you serve as a Navajo Code Talker"? Kenji explained to my grandfather that he was writing a book about Navajo Code Talkers and discussed the process.

My grandfather replied, "War was bad, and I don't feel like talking about it".

He shook Kenji's hand and went back to his tractor. My grandmother explained to Kenji that grandfather does not talk about his war experience, and we never pressure him to speak about it.

Kenji was a nice and understanding guy. He passed along his contact information and asked my grandmother to contact him if my grandfather changed his mind. Kenji did publish his book which highlights different Navajo Code Talkers throughout the Navajo Reservation.

Grandfather did not feel comfortable speaking with people of Japanese ancestry due to his involvement in the South Asian War Theatre. I got the sense that he had some type of underlying fear and trauma associated with Japanese people. To address this trauma, my grandfather chose to not speak of his war experience and felt it was healthier to leave the memories in the past.

My undergraduate studies were completed at Fort Lewis College in Durango, Colorado. In our apartment, we had an electronic monitor set up in which we had to charge a credit card at the power company. Once credits were added to the card, it was swiped on the monitor in the apartment. If credits dropped to zero on the apparatus, we were charged a large fee.

During the long breaks, my Japanese roommate went back to Japan. My grandparents' home phone number was given to him in the event of an emergency. For the Christmas break, my time was spent working double shifts as a dishwasher at a Mexican Restaurant to save money for the next semester which left little time for me to be at my apartment.

Masaaki, my Japanese roommate, would leave messages on our phone and was worried when his calls were not returned. So, he called my grandparents' home. Grandfather answered the phone and was surprised to receive a phone call from Japan.

The last time grandfather had a meaningful conversation with someone of Japanese ancestry was when he entered Okinawa with the Marines. Since that time, my grandfather avoided speaking with Japanese people due to the trauma associated with the war.

Given that Masaaki called out of concern, grandfather was willing to speak with him. In my opinion, the innocent phone conversation opened a line of dialogue and ultimately a path to healing for him.

On my days off, my refuge was smoking expensive cigars and pretending to be rich. My grandparents rolled up to my apartment in their truck and were dressed up. I should have known something was up because they typically do not leave their home unless it was important.

Grandfather opened the door to his truck and stepped out with his shiny cowboy boots, pressed shirt, new jeans, and turquoise stone watch. Grandmother wore her dressy clothing along with turquoise beads, bracelets, and rings. Initially, I thought they were coming to inform me of a death in the family.

Grandmother specified, "Grandpa got a phone call from Japan. Someone named Masaaki talked to Grandpa and left this number for you to call him. He said you can call collect; he just wants to know if you've been adding credits to the power box."

She handed me a piece of paper with my roommate's name,

international number, and a security code to make a collect call.

"Yes, I've been keeping up with the credits and I will call him back," I assured her.

"I got a call from your Japanese friend. He was a nice guy. I have not talked to anyone from Japan in a long time," Grandfather replied.

I burned myself trying to extinguish the cigar so as not to smoke in front of my grandparents. Expensive cigars were something I enjoyed while dreaming of someday making it big and landing a career.

Grandfather asked me in Navajo, "What are you smoking? Are you trying to be a Medicine Man?" His eyes crinkled at the edges as he gently teased me for my vice.

Utilizing a large tobacco smoke device was typically associated with being a medicine man. Tobacco smoke was viewed as an offering to the Holy People and less of enjoyment.

When I think back on that time, I smile. Maybe I should've been a medicine man. I certainly needed that kind of wisdom for the next leg of my journey.

# CHAPTER 19

*The Tó'aheedlíinii Lady pretended to sleep as her son brought the horses through the canyon. The old rocky caverns were like natural cathedrals in the late afternoon sun. She marveled over the animal skeletons littering the ground. Some were polished smooth by the sandstorms she remembered wreaking havoc on her father's village at least once or twice a year.*

*Capture her... Kill her.*

*She looked fearfully over her shoulder, searching the horizon for the invaders that longed to take her life all those years ago. For as far as she traveled, the circle was nearly complete. Being home wasn't a choice it was a necessity. Her leap of faith had taken her far, but there was one last task to be done.*

In adulthood, nightmares developed due to my traumatized childhood. Thinking back about my childhood, I realize that my father was exposed to domestic violence and alcohol usage at an early age which shaped his behavior as an adult. From the beginning, he had the cards stacked against him and was fighting an uphill battle. Without making an excuse for my father, he had his learning and emotional well-being disrupted at an early age. However, it was my choice to forgive my father.

His trauma-based behaviors and actions had to be distinguished and understood as it was learned behavior he picked up as a child. When people are exposed to repeated trauma as children, it somehow negatively programs their brains. By taking an empathic perspective, my father had his issues to address.

This encouraged me to take the position to stop blaming my father for my past problems. But instead, taking responsibility and ownership of myself. As an adult, it was my responsibility to stop the cycle of violence and not allow my children to experience trauma.

My father's mother was an alcoholic. So, he had early exposure to domestic violence and alcoholism. As an adult, it took a long time to understand my father's absence, and to become empathic to his lifestyle.

In 2006, a phone call was made to my grandmother that my father was a John Doe at the University of New Mexico Healthcare Center. He was found after having a seizure in a back alley in Albuquerque, New Mexico.

Ultimately, the choice was to forgive my father but it was a challenge. Every reason existed to forget about my father, allowing him to become a ward of the state. A hospital social worker spoke with me and indicated it would be easier to become a surrogate guardian for my father. With the hospital social worker's help, a rehabilitation center was secured. Being my father's guardian involved applying for Medicaid and Social Security.

Luckily, my training as a clinical counselor and school psychologist gave me the technical knowledge to fill out the application. Whenever something went down with him, the nursing staff called me which took time away from my work and doctoral schoolwork.

Having taken the responsibility for my father and becoming his surrogate guardian was a difficult undertaking. It is not easy forgiving your attacker and abuser, then being his or her guardian.

"Your father will need long-term care after he is finished at the UNM-Hospital," the social worker said.

"How long will it take you to get him a room?"

"For your father to become a ward of the state is a long process because he has been deemed mentally incompetent to take care of himself."

"What does it mean when someone is mentally incompetent?"

"When a person is considered mentally incompetent," she replied. "That means they are unable to take care of themselves and can't live independently. So, we can't release your father to be on his own, he needs to be in a home living care facility."

"After speaking with the doctors, we are hoping you would be able to become your father's surrogate guardian because it would make finding him a facility easier. Also, he will need to apply for Medicaid which you can do for him," she said. "So, are you willing to become your father's surrogate?"

In my mind, that was a loaded question and my life flashed before my eyes. At that point, a decision had to be made whether the care of my father became my ultimate responsibility. I had to set aside my trauma and help the man that caused it.

Instead of the abusive and neglectful, I had to see my father as he was, a frail broken man that was in dire need of my help. At that moment, my thoughts centered on the Ranger Creed in which you will never leave a fallen comrade to fall into the hands of the enemy.

"All right, what do I need to do?"

The thought quickly occurred to me what kind of mess taking on my father's care would involve. A shred of doubt entered my mind but was quickly erased after seeing the reaction of the social worker as she smiled and presented with a sigh of relief.

"Okay, I'll get you the Medicaid application and start checking into facilities for your father," she said.

"You're doing a very noble thing agreeing to take responsibility for your father. I understand his situation of being homeless and know they don't have much contact with their family. A few weeks ago, a family was in the same situation, and they flat out said 'no' and then walked away."

We stood there near the front entrance of the hospital as we conversed. Although a lot of people were entering and exiting the hospital, we were in a quiet confidential section which people passing could not easily hear us. The hospital was grey on the outside but presented with a standard white 'hospital color'. The scent inside was the same rubbery scent present in most hospitals. Across from where we conversed, a deli was filled with people partaking in a decent meal.

While walking back up to my father's hospital room, a feeling of doubt circulated in my mind. However, the social worker was right about being my father's guardian was a noble move. She did not know about the abuse, alcoholism, and domestic violence, associated with my father and I did not tell her.

When speaking with the hospital social worker, it was not the correct time to confide in her. Rather than spilling the beans about my issues, it was better to focus on my father's health.

Sitting in the hospital bed, father gave off a roar as he was being held down. My father was like a grizzly bear who did not want to be caged and stay in the hospital. At one point, the hospital staff had father strapped into his bed because of his combative nature. Not only that, but father was detoxing from constantly having alcohol in his system.

"Your father keeps fighting us as we tried feeding and giving him food. We tried to hold your father down, but it did not work," the nurse said.

"Get me the hell out of here! These people won't let me go!"

"Hey dad, these people are trying to help you. They told me you were found downtown behind a building," I said to my father.

"Do you know who I am?" I asked my father. With a puzzled and unshaven face, Father looked hard trying to recognize me.

"Son, is that you?" he asked, staring at me with equal parts wonder and disbelief on his grizzled features.

"Yes, it's me and I'm here to help out. They want to transfer you to a facility," I replied. Gone was the black hair and the matching cowboy hat. The alcohol had robbed him of his youth and what few memories he had left.

"Why take me there? I want to go back to the Good Shepard."

I almost laughed. Good Shepard was a homeless shelter located in downtown Albuquerque, which provides food and temporary shelter to transient people.

Alcohol addiction still has a stronghold given it causes physiological and mental cravings. So, for my father, he needed that drink to settle his nerves and restore his bodily functions. After constant drinking, the body has difficulty functioning without alcohol.

As I prepared to bring him home, all I could think about was the years of pain and fear. Had he been a younger man still in control of his faculties, I dreamed that one day I would finally have it out with him. I would tell him how badly he hurt me and how angry I was that he checked out of my life when I needed him most. I would remind him of the fear and the rage and all of the times and ways he broke our family by choosing his addiction over us. I'd scream, rage, and pour out all the pent-up malice that poisoned my soul all those years.

As I looked at that pitiful man in that bed, I did the one thing I thought I would never do. I helped him dress, then took him home.

# CHAPTER 20

*The Tó'aheedlíinii Lady straightened the cloak around her frail body.*

*"What if he does not make it, mother? The sun will be rising soon. If he is caught sleeping," her son warned.*

*She looked toward the horizon and tilted her head.*

*"Hush now. He will come."*

When people experience a significant amount of trauma, they have a choice of continuing or stopping the cycle. In terms of personal empowerment, my hope is more people would take a positive position when it comes to dealing with their trauma. The cycle does not have to be passed on to the younger generations. We have the power to make positive choices to better ourselves.

Navajo people have important teaching called T'áá hwó' ají t'éego which means "It is up to you to live a productive life." The translation dictates that we must take the initiative to make life good for ourselves and learn to be self-sufficient. No matter how hard life becomes, we must roll up our sleeves and put in the work to address our issues. Most of my uncles were military veterans and medicine men, but they were all of the same mind.

*Nephew, at some point you have to do things for yourself. You have two hands, use them to earn money and make a living for yourself. You have a good career, take care of it. When we are no longer around, it's your paycheck that's going to sustain and allow you to take care of your children. Don't just go hang around a women's house, do nothing, and live off handouts. That's not the Navajo way.*

At some point, you must take responsibility for your actions. Life is based on the choices that we make. Whichever choice we make, we must own it and take responsibility for our actions.

We cannot control what other people do and how they think of us. Hence, we can only control ourselves and our path in life. It takes maturity and knowledge to understand this concept. This information can only be learned through trial and tribulations and overcoming them. This allows us to understand "who we are" as people. We must learn how to survive and thrive. Overall, life itself becomes our teacher.

Life is difficult, but it makes us stronger. We can sit there feeling sorry for ourselves, but that never solves anything. When we don't do anything productive, life passes us by. Once we have accomplished something very important, we need to feel proud and own it. For example, once we acquire an academic degree of some sort, whether it be an associate to a doctorate, that becomes ours. Nobody can ever take that away from you.

In Navajo culture, we were taught to have reverence for one another and the environment. We are interconnected, and each is relative and relevant. We have a deep sense of respect for the earth and other elements. Hence, we belong to the land and have a relationship with all of nature. The mother is our Earth, and the father is the Sky. All animals are our relatives, and we have respect for them.

Running is a large part of indigenous life and culture which allows the reconnection with mother earth and nature. Running in the morning has the same significance as morning prayer and the brain is free to think. In consideration of the runner's ability, he or she makes a sacrifice through their suffering. The Holy People look down and acknowledge the runner as it relates to their prayers.

When a young person runs, they are following the practices of The Hero Twins. In most mythology, warrior archetypes exist. For example, in Greek mythology, Hercules plays that role. In Navajo culture, we have the hero twins called Monster Slayer and Born for the Water. During that time, monsters ruled the earth making life difficult for the five-fingered people.

The Hero Twins made a journey to the sun, their father, to acquire the weapons necessary to fight the monsters. Once the Hero Twins reach the sun, they underwent a series of tests to prove they were the offspring of the sun. After passing the required tests, they were given weapons to rid the earth of the monsters. The Hero Twins killed most monsters to make it safe for humans to emerge from the underworld.

Navajo puberty ceremonies called the Kinaldaa are a testament to those prayers. During the ceremony, a girl goes through an initiation process to become a woman. The ceremony typically lasts for four days. Each morning the female participant runs as far as she can with her family. A female deity called Changing Woman was the first participant to experience the Kinaldaa ceremony.

Typically, it takes me the first mile to start enjoying the process of running. The first mile sucks since the brain and body is telling me to stop. After my body gets warmed up and the adrenaline starts to flow, then it feels good and also feels as though I can go forever. The same way as overcoming obstacles and challenges and coming out the other side, victorious and ready to run the next leg of the journey.

Live your life. You only get one.

# CHAPTER 21

*In dreams, we are luminous beings. We are the twins. We are changing women and the walls of the canyons rising like a cathedral into the clouds. In dreams, I am a man walking the path The Tó'aheedlíinii Lady ran. Sometimes I am running alongside her fighting off the invaders, dodging the addiction and the despair that kept my parents bound.*

*The muscles in my legs ache, but I continue to run forward, forever forward as I see my children take their first wobbly steps into adulthood. I pass the man I was and revel at the streaks of grey and the laugh lines on the face of the man I choose to be.*

*I wave at my grandparents and uncles as the canyon floor becomes fields of alfalfa and vines hanging heavy with zucchini. The air filling my lungs sings of the mud and the sage bushes kissed by the rain. I run with the horses racing out of the sun as the songs of the medicine men and the Holy People flow in and out of me with each breath. Farther and faster, I run until all that is left is the wind and the smell of clay and spices.*

*And then I look to the top of the canyon and see a lone figure standing high against the new dawn. Her black hair ripples like an ocean of midnight and her red dress shimmers like the sun. I scale the first level and the thousands to follow, never slipping, never tiring, and then she is gone.*

As an Indigenous writer, it is difficult to revisit and talk about trauma. To progress and grow, we—I needed to look inward and learn to make peace with myself. By writing this book, it has turned into the journey of a lifetime. The day I stopped blaming my parents and other people for my failures was the first of a thousand steps. The rest of the race is what we—what I—make it.

It is possible to let go of the past and allow your mind to heal from trauma. The human mind is capable of healing itself beyond our level of understanding. I chose to pass on positive knowledge and to support my amazing and beautiful wife and brilliant and resourceful sons to the best of my ability. My oldest son, Preston, is studying civil engineering at the New Mexico Institute of Mining and Technology which is one of the Nation's top STEM schools.

Growing up, my mother and father did not provide me with a strong foundation in the Navajo language. It is easy to feel upset and "robbed" for not being thoroughly taught the Navajo language or culture, but all is not lost. Currently, there is a strong push to preserve and maintain the Navajo language and culture which is based on oral presentation and tradition. For this reason, the Navajo language and culture were passed down by oral means versus written form. Only recently has the Navajo language been written in text format. Even so, few people can interpret the language. Having the ability to do so involves being able to understand basic word structures in written Navajo which is completely different from English-based words.

Still, I'm grateful because it's a start; a damn fine one. This can only grow if we turn on the water of enlightenment to wash away the stain of ignorance. If we irrigate the barren land of childhood trauma with compassion and forgiveness. If we tend as carefully to our youth as I did those horses and vegetable gardens when I was a boy, then we can chart a peaceful path to healing.

We are standing on fertile ground with hearts filled with seeds. If we pour into our children and our society, the songs and stories that fill our souls can replenish our culture. We are no longer the product of our trauma. We are proof of our ancestors' dreams are ... alive and thriving.

We must remember our roots and where we came from. It is easy to get stuck in this "poor me" attitude. Our ancestors went through tougher times, and we owe it to them to keep pushing forward. The victim mentality must be conquered to overcome obstacles. No matter how tough life is, we must keep moving forward.

As Navajo people, we are resilient people having survived forced relocation and captivity.

We are the descendants of The Tó'aheedlíinii Lady and all that came before her. We were built to last.

*The Tó'aheedlíinii Lady took in a breath and warmed her face in the rays of the sun. He was close now. The sounds of his feet thundered in her blood. Every step brought him out of the trauma and closer to his destiny. He fell along the way as they all did from time to time, but he got up. He pushed on. For some years he slowed down. Other times, he stopped, but he was close now; so close.*

*She opened her eyes and looked at her son and all of the sons and daughters standing beyond him outnumbering the stars.*

*"Do you see him, mother?"*

*"He is here. Darryl is here."*

*The Tó'aheedlíinii Lady nodded as her gaze drifted to a younger version of herself extending a hand. As their spirits merged, she moved to the mouth of the canyon. He glanced over his shoulder, and she helped him to the top.*

*All of her hopes ... of her dreams and prayers shimmered in his eyes.*

*She embraced him like an old friend.*

*Welcome home, Darryl. You made it.*

*Free Range Love* by Darryl Benally

Kevin is a rancher with a love for the land and Navajo tradition. Shanice is a city girl with a broken heart and a fondness for shopping. The one thing they have in common is the time they served in the military, when a potential relationship never took root. After reuniting three years later, what will it take to rekindle the spark that stalled before it could ignite? One week on a ranch in Nevada might be enough to bring them together…or will their differences return and tear them apart?

The sun rose gently over the horizon, eager to warm the early spring morning. Delicate, white frost dusted the ground. As warmth returned, soft steam drifted upward from the earth like dancing ghosts celebrating the start of the planting season. The Bahe Family land, nestled between the mountains and acres of lush greenery, had been in Kevin's family for centuries.

The day started off well enough. However, in his dreams, his lady ancestor warned him of chaos. Then he heard it. The sound that every rancher dreaded. Massive hoof beats heading in the wrong direction. Loud enough to vibrate through the entire house.

Kevin Bahe yanked back the woven comforter, ran from the bed, and scooped up a pair of jeans and a white cotton shirt. He slid into his clothes as he bypassed the guest quarters, den, and living and dining rooms only to find Shanice Johnson sitting at the breakfast table nursing a cup of coffee. His grandparents were nowhere to be seen.

"What's going on?" she asked, abandoning her coffee to stand, giving his muscular form a quick once-over. "Why are you dressed for outside?"

"One of my knucklehead cousins left the gate open, and the cows escaped. I need to round them up before they make it to the road, or we'll be eating beef every single day for the next ten years. I've been hearing a lot about smash burgers, but this wasn't the way I wanted to try them."

He was ticked with a capital T because the cousins—Knuckleheads One and Two—only came around when they wanted money. Instead of allowing them to take advantage of his grandparents' generosity, Kevin assigned them tasks at the ranch and made them work for pay. They resented it, though they would make substantially more money and wouldn't need handouts. Unfortunately, this latest episode of negligence was why he didn't trust them to run the ranch. Kevin had to split his time between the ranch and his demanding child psychology practice because they'd already shown they couldn't be trusted with little things.

"How can I help?" Shanice asked, grabbing her coat from the back of the wooden chair.

"You can't," he said, making his way to the threshold of the back yard. "At least not with this."

She flinched, and he realized his words sounded harsher than he intended. Probably because the woman who showed up for a visit was a totally different woman than the one he met while he was in the Army and she was in the Air Force. He had asked her to bring comfortable clothing—jeans, tees, sneakers and such. He saw that she'd disregarded that suggestion when exotic luggage was rolling behind her, about five deep for a week-long visit to his ranch on the Navajo reservation. A far cry from the woman who'd carried a duffle bag and went on parachute jumps during airborne operations.

"I've slept the entire week," Shanice said. "I need to do something."

"We need help in the garden."

Shanice grimaced. "I don't have a green thumb, I have a black one. Anything I touch dies."

Kevin gave a heavy sigh. "How about bailing the hay?"

"You want me to do what? Horses? Manure?" She glanced down at her designer clothes then back up at him. "I really don't want to ruin them. Didn't I see some list on the fridge that said something about putting a sheep in the staging area? That sounds real simple."

"You can't do that," he said, glancing over his shoulder to see if his grandfather had made it to the front of the house.

"It's just one sheep, right? I mean, if King David handled a whole flock…"

"He was a trained professional. He also killed a lion and a bear with his bare hands. The only thing you know about sheep is lamb chops and gyros."

"I know they're responsible for the best fuzzy socks. Also feta cheese! Have you ever had feta? It's just—"

He turned back to her. "Shanice, I'm not going to debate about this. No."

She folded her arms over her bosom, and if eyes were daggers, he'd be pinned to the wall. He ignored her and walked out the door before he became a prime candidate for a pin-the-tale-on-the-donkey game with him being the unfortunate donkey.

This version of her still had the same beautiful inside, but the exterior never went anywhere without a full covering of cosmetics, designer clothes, hair swept up in an elegant style—full-on Hollywood red carpet glam. The Dolce & Gabbana sweater embraced her curves like a well-fitted glove; the Versace washed jeans were so tight it looked like she'd been poured into them. But it was the suede boots from the land of Prada that were going to give her the most grief. The ranch was no place for being cute; it was for folks who were practical.

"I have to do something." She was right behind him, footsteps crunching on the grass. "I'm going crazy out of my mind doing nothing here."

Kevin slowed his steps since she was determined to keep up. "All right. You want to do something helpful?" He scooped up a rope that had been left in the grass. "We'll do it together. When I get back."

She gazed at the rope like he just handed her a toddler who needed a diaper change. "I don't know what to do with this."

"Then how, exactly, were you going to help me with the cattle?"

"I planned to … watch," she said, shrugging. "Provide moral support. Cheer you on from a safe distance. Pray?"

Kevin chuckled and snatched the rope, preparing to toss it back toward the pen. "Then you'll need to stay in the house until I get back. I think a Kevin Bacon marathon is on. Footloose is my favorite."

"I'm not doing that," she snapped, holding out a hand for the rope. "It's not like I haven't been on a farm before, Kevin. I spent summers down south with my grandparents. One sheep. Into a pen. I'll get it done."

"In heels and designer duds?" he asked, picking up speed after surveying the damage and realizing the cows had a pretty good head start. The minute he laid eyes on the knuckleheads he was going to pop them upside the head. "Shanice, at what point did you think that high heels, mud, and grassy fields were going to be a perfect combination? Mario Prada is rolling in his grave right now. Or is it Luigi?"

"You're thinking of the video game," she said in a sour tone. "But that fact that you put Mario and Prada in the same sentence means you know a little something, something."

"Yes, I do. Like none of them, Prada, Gucci, Versace belong on the range."

He was used to this woman feeling comfortable in jeans, T-shirt, sneakers, maybe a dusting of cosmetics. He didn't know what happened to her since he last saw her three years ago. This week she had mostly slept, and she missed so many meals that his grandma was concerned. When had her obsession with designer clothes and material things begun? Even the pajamas were Dolce. She hadn't worn nearly one-hundredth of the clothes she had brought.

Now, two days before she was set to leave, she was genuinely eager to contribute and earn the respect of Kevin's grandparents. This had been a challenge for her, as she grew up with all the convenient trappings of city life. An Air Force background, military and self-defense training, and the fact that she'd been competitive in both college volleyball and basketball were probably good points, but not enough to justify her high-heeled Prada boots being drafted to engage in hand-to-hoof combat with a wooly, 150-pound mood swing.

Unfortunately, she'd been learning that life on the reservation was a different kind of experience. People lived close to nature, relied on livestock and their gardens for food, and depended on each other for everything else. It could be isolating for those who craved the excitement and convenience the city provided. She couldn't wrap her head around Chick-fil-A not being hand-delivered directly to the ranch by an Uber Eats virtuoso.

"I promise we'll do it together when I get back," Kevin said, placing a hand over hers, relishing the soft brown skin and citrus scent.

"When will that be?"

"Not sure, but the longer I'm talking to you, the longer it'll take."

"All right, I got this," she said, squaring her shoulders and looking every bit as confident as he remembered. "You worry about the cows, and I'll worry about the sheep. Deal?"

Kevin looked at Shanice, knowing how stubborn she was. But since the highway was close, he had to act quickly. He didn't want any of his grandparents' valuable cattle harmed; they were an important source of income. Besides, if a vehicle hit one of them, the vehicle's damage would be substantial. Smash burgers and lawsuits.

With a determined expression, Shanice winked and gave him a reassuring smile. "Oh, ye of little faith."

"It's not my faith I'm worried about." He was fully aware that she didn't have a clue what she was about to get into, but knowing her track record, she'd improvise to power through.

Shanice gazed at the rope in her beautifully manicured hands.

Those won't last an hour.

He whispered a prayer of gratefulness for the sheep. Also for their cooperation.

Shanice tightened her grip on the rope and shrugged. "Just like when we rappelled off the high tower with ropes back in the military."

"Ever heard the saying that a hard head makes a soft ass?"

"Just one sheep, right?"

He could feel her eyes on him as he ran to the stables, hopped on a horse, situated himself in the saddle, then aimed to catch up with his grandfather riding just past the fence. The two of them made a beeline east toward the main road.

Kevin glanced over his shoulder at Shanice. That woman just won't listen. This is going to be the most humbling experience of her life. Too bad I won't be able to watch.

*Free Range Love* is one of the amazing stories in Rom-Complications, an anthology featuring *New York Times* Bestselling Author Steven Barnes, *USA Today* Bestselling Author Naleighna Kai, and many others.

# ABOUT THE AUTHOR

Darryl Benally is a Navajo author, school psychologist, mental health therapist, and Army veteran who resides in New Mexico and Arizona. Darryl has a Doctor of Education degree from New Mexico State University. He owns a consulting business called Warrior Psychological Consulting, LLC and primarily works on the Navajo Reservation. His love of literary writing began when he joined NK's Tribe Called Success.

Reading, traveling, spending time with family, and trail running is what he most enjoys when not putting pen to paper.

Visit Darryl on the web:

Sociatap: https://sociatap.com/darrylbenally
Email: dhbenally@gmail.com